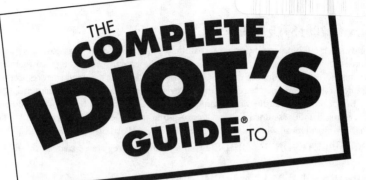

THE COMPLETE IDIOT'S GUIDE® TO

Yorkshire Terriers

by Liz Palika

ALPHA

A Pearson Education Company

Copyright © 2003 by Liz Palika

International Standard Book Number: 0-02-864458-1
Library of Congress Catalog Card Number: 2002115721

04 03 02   8 7 6 5 4 3 2 1

Interpretation of the printing code: The rightmost number of the first series of numbers is the year of the book's printing; the rightmost number of the second series of numbers is the number of the book's printing. For example, a printing code of 02-1 shows that the first printing occurred in 2002.

Printed in the United States of America

Note: This publication contains the opinions and ideas of its author. It is intended to provide helpful and informative material on the subject matter covered. It is sold with the understanding that the author and publisher are not engaged in rendering professional services in the book. If the reader requires personal assistance or advice, a competent professional should be consulted.

The author and publisher specifically disclaim any responsibility for any liability, loss, or risk, personal or otherwise, which is incurred as a consequence, directly or indirectly, of the use and application of any of the contents of this book.

For marketing and publicity, please call: 317-581-3722

The publisher offers discounts on this book when ordered in quantity for bulk purchases and special sales.

For sales within the United States, please contact: Corporate and Government Sales, 1-800-382-3419 or corpsales@pearsontechgroup.com

Outside the United States, please contact: International Sales, 317-581-3793 or international@pearsontechgroup.com

Publisher: *Marie Butler-Knight*
Product Manager: *Phil Kitchel*
Managing Editor: *Jennifer Chisholm*
Senior Acquisitions Editor: *Mike Sanders*
Development Editor: *Jennifer Moore*
Copy Editor: *Cari Luna*
Illustrator: *Chris Eliopoulos*
Cover/Book Designer: *Trina Wurst*
Indexer: *Julie Bess*
Layout/Proofreading: *Becky Harmon, Vicki Keller*

Permission to reprint the Yorkshire Terrier Breed Standard in Chapter 2 granted by the Yorkshire Terrier Club of America.

All photographs by Ed Kelley.

Contents at a Glance

Contents

Foreword

The Yorkshire Terrier, although small in stature, is actually a multi-talented breed. Commonly referred to as the "Yorkie," this is an energetic, smart, athletic, and feisty dog. Unfortunately, this cute yet spirited dog is frequently misunderstood and often underestimated. In *The Complete Idiot's Guide to Yorkshire Terriers*, author Liz Palika does an excellent job of explaining where and how to choose a Yorkie puppy. And she gives an in-depth overview about the true nature and needs of Yorkies while dispelling some of the ugly little myths that exist about small dogs, and Yorkies in particular.

For example, although Yorkies are small and light enough to sit on your lap, don't be misled into thinking that they should be content to sit on your lap all day. Although the AKC categorizes the Yorkie as a "Toy" breed, when you get a Yorkie, you're getting a true terrier, bred to be a hunter and killer of small vermin (think rats and mice). Yorkies have a high prey drive and major determination—they are tenacious and are bred not to give up. They can play fetch for hours, shine in dog sports, and excel at obedience.

People often mistakenly believe that because Yorkies are small, they don't need to be trained. Not only do Yorkies need to be trained, they thrive on it! It's not unusual in a group class for the Yorkie to be the star student—they can steal the show. Know this: If you don't train your Yorkie, your Yorkie will train you!

Small dogs still have big needs—and the operative word here is *dog*. Over the last 16 years as a dog trainer and behavioral consultant, at least once a week a client expresses concern to me about his or her Yorkie's hyperactivity, mouthing, housetraining, barking, or fearfulness. The first thing I always ask is "How much exercise does your Yorkie get every day?" Invariably, the answer is "My dog is a house dog, so I don't take him outside." There is no such thing as a "house dog." I regretfully tell them that if they wanted a pet to remain in the house, they should have gotten a fish. I try to hide my anger and sadness over this poor dog who is leading a boring and unnatural life.

Yorkies are an exceedingly popular breed. But being popular is a double-edge sword in the world of dogs. With their increased popularity, Yorkies are too easy to obtain. Take our advice and stay away from pet stores and backyard breeders. These little guys, when bred by nonprofessionals, are often fraught with poor temperament and ill health, which then leads to uncharacteristic traits in the breed such as anxiety, fearfulness, aggression, and obsessive-compulsive disorder, not to mention aberrations in the size of the breed such as being too small or too large. So be careful. A good breeder won't try to convince you to get a dog, but will interview *you* to determine if you and the breed make a good fit. Buying a dog is always a business transaction! Do it with someone you can trust. And remember this: No good or reputable dog breeder will sell to a store—there are no exceptions!

Intelligence and cuteness are equally matched in the Yorkshire terrier. In *The Complete Idiot's Guide to Yorkshire Terriers*, Liz Palika will enlighten and educate you about all you will need to know about choosing, raising, training, and just having fun with your new family member.

Congratulations, and enjoy the new relationship.

Stacy Alldredge
Owner, Who's Walking Who Dog Obedience and
Behavioral Training
212-414-1551
wwwdogs@aol.com

Introduction

The Complete Idiot's Guide to Yorkshire Terriers is not like most of the breed books you've seen. Most breed books are written by judges, exhibitors, and breeders of that particular breed, and they will tell you how spectacular that breed is. In those books you can read about winning show dogs and see photographs of champion dogs. You can hear the awesome characteristics of that breed and how it could be the best choice for everyone. Well, this book isn't like those books.

As a dog obedience instructor, I see more than 700 dogs and their owners each year in my classes. Many of the new dog owners have done a lot of research before adding a dog to their family, and yet they still find out their research has not been complete. They really didn't know as much about the breed as they had thought.

This book will help you decide whether you should get a dog—any dog—and whether you have the time, energy, and money to take care of one. Once you have made a decision about dog ownership, then you can decide whether a Yorkshire Terrier is the right breed for you and your family. You may find that a Yorkie sounds perfect for you, or you may decide that a Yorkie wouldn't fit into your lifestyle at all. And if that's the situation, well, it's best to find that out *before* you bring one home!

Once you figure out if a Yorkie is the right dog for you, Part 2 will show you how to prepare for your new family member and what to do once you bring home your new Yorkie. You'll find out all about housetraining and establishing some household rules. Of course, you'll want to know how to take care of your Yorkie, and Part 3 will help you learn how to groom your dog and how to care for him, including some emergency first-aid information. Part 4 will guide you through the training process and also answer common questions about training and canine behavior.

This book is written for people who are thinking of adding a Yorkie to their family or who already have a Yorkie but want to better understand him.

Who Am I?

As a dog obedience instructor with more than 25 years of experience, I have watched many Yorkie owners come into class carrying their dog because the dog has repeatedly refused to walk on a leash. There are usually housetraining problems, many times the dog is biting or nipping, and he is usually being fed from the table. Sometimes there have been complaints from neighbors that the dog is barking nonstop when the owner leaves the house. Are Yorkies really this horrible? Well, they shouldn't be, but they can be!

I teach dog obedience classes because I love dogs and enjoy sharing my life with them. My husband and I enjoy many different activities with our dogs, but we also treasure quiet times at home with them. Our dogs are good friends and companions. However, when a dog turns into a tyrant and makes life miserable, he is no longer a joy to spend time with.

When dog owners understand why their dogs do what they do, they can then either change the situation or learn to live with it. However, when dog owners do not understand their dogs, the levels of anger and frustration can escalate until the dog is no longer a member of the family and is discarded. My goal is to make sure dog owners realize they have a means of making sure their dog is a friend and companion rather than a tyrant!

I have taught all levels of dog obedience, from puppy through the advanced obedience classes, called utility. However, my primary focus is teaching pet owners how to train their dogs to be well-behaved members of the family, and I have found this to be extremely rewarding. When someone enrolls in one of my classes and says, "I took your classes 14 years ago with my dog, Roxie. She was a wonderful dog but just passed away. When we got a new puppy, we wanted her to go through your training, so she will be a good dog, too!" Well, then all my efforts have paid off!

Decoding the Text

You don't need to be an expert on dogs or Yorkshire Terriers to understand this book. There will be no technical gibberish of any kind, and any words I feel need to be defined, will be!

You will find four different kinds of sidebars throughout this book, each designed to add some additional information to the text.

Yorkie Smarts
This advice will help you be a smart Yorkie owner.

Watch Out!
Careful! These tips are important.

Bet You Didn't Know
Dogs can be puzzling to humans sometimes, and this information will help you to better understand them.

Dog Talk
These doggy definitions will make understanding this book a walk in the park!

Special Thanks to the Technical Reviewer

The Complete Idiot's Guide to Yorkshire Terriers was reviewed by an expert who double-checked the accuracy of what you'll learn here, to help us ensure that this book gives you everything you need to know about Yorkshire Terriers. Special thanks are extended to Deb Eldredge, a dog owner, competitor, and veterinarian, and Beth Adelman, an experienced dog book editor and the former editor of *DogWorld* and the *AKC Gazette*.

Trademarks

All terms mentioned in this book that are known to be or are suspected of being trademarks or service marks have been appropriately capitalized. Alpha Books and Pearson Education, Inc., cannot attest to the accuracy of this information. Use of a term in this book should not be regarded as affecting the validity of any trademark or service mark.

Part 1

The King of Terriers

A dog—even a tiny one—is a big responsibility. So before you bring home a dog, take a good hard look at what's involved in dog ownership. Make sure you will have the time, money, and energy to care for a dog for his or her lifetime.

If you decide that a dog would suit your needs and lifestyle and that you will be able to care for one properly, it's time to look at Yorkshire Terriers. Yorkies are tiny dogs with the heart of a king—they don't know they are small! We'll look at what makes Yorkies so special, and we'll see if a Yorkie is the right breed for you.

Where do you find a Yorkie? We'll take a look at breeders, rescue groups, and other ways of finding a dog, and we'll discuss the pros and cons of each. Then we'll consider how to choose the right dog for you. The Yorkie you buy or adopt will depend on you for all its care and companionship and will be your best friend, so let's make sure you choose the best dog for you.

Chapter 1

Is a Yorkshire Terrier the Right Dog for You?

In This Chapter

- The responsibility of owning a dog
- Considering your money, time, and energy
- The pros and cons of dog ownership
- Getting to know Yorkies

Yorkshire Terriers, usually called "Yorkies," are very attractive, appealing, tiny dogs. Classified as toy breed dogs by the American Kennel Club (AKC) rather than terriers, Yorkies are treasured by toy dog fanciers as well as people who enjoy terriers.

The popularity of Yorkies has remained constant for many years. The AKC's statistics for 2001 showed Yorkies as the sixth most popular breed, with more than 40,000 dogs registered. The United Kennel Club (UKC), which classifies the breed as a Companion Dog (rather than a toy breed), ranks the Yorkshire Terrier as the

seventeenth most popular breed out of the 300 breeds recognized by that registry.

People who treasure Yorkies like the breed for a variety of reasons. Some enjoy the breed's tiny size while others enjoy the terrier temperament. No matter what appeals to them, people who love Yorkies do so enthusiastically. This tiny "King of Terriers" has a devoted following.

Dog Ownership Is a Responsibility

Recently in one of my dog training classes, the owner of a young Yorkie puppy admitted to me that when she bought her puppy, she had no idea how much work a puppy required. A wife, mother, and career woman, she thought a puppy would fit into her family with little fuss. Instead, within days, she found out that having a puppy was almost like having another child!

Luckily for this Yorkie puppy, his owner and her family have made the commitment to make the situation work. They love the puppy and even though they have a busy lifestyle, all have accepted the responsibility to do what is right for the puppy. Unfortunately, not everyone is so dedicated. Many dogs end up in rescue or in shelters because their owners didn't realize what dog ownership entails.

Dog Talk

Yorkies originated in Scotland and England and the name Yorkshire Terrier comes from Yorkshire, England.

Before deciding whether a Yorkie is the right breed for you, you should ask yourself whether you should even have a dog. Dog ownership isn't for everyone. Have you had other dogs? Did those dogs live out their lives with you? If they did, wonderful! If they didn't, why not? A dog should be a lifetime commitment.

Have you had other pets? Cats, rabbits, hamsters, or tropical fish? Did those pets live their lives with you? Did you responsibly keep the litter box, cage, or aquarium clean?

If you have kept pets previously and were willing to do what was needed to keep them healthy and happy, and the pets lived out their lives with you, dog ownership might well be the right choice for you. However, if you have the habit of giving up a pet when things get tough, or if you're not willing to do dirty chores (there *will* be messes), then please rethink the idea of getting a dog.

Watch Out!

Dog ownership is more than wet kisses and a warm body cuddled next to you on the sofa. Dog ownership is also a number of chores that must be done daily. Can you do those chores without fail?

The popularity of Yorkies has remained stable for the past decade.

A Dog Isn't Inexpensive

It's a very good idea to take a look at your budget before adding a dog to your household. Many people have no idea how much dog ownership really costs. A good-quality Yorkshire Terrier from a reputable breeder will not be cheap, although prices do vary. A dog from a Yorkie rescue group may cost less but will still require a donation to the group. A Yorkie from a shelter will also require a donation.

You'll also need to do some shopping for your new dog. He'll need a crate, dog food, a collar and leash, and some toys. You should get a baby gate or two for your house, and you may need to do some work on your backyard fence. You may also need to build a dog run.

Ongoing expenses will include dog food, visits to the veterinarian, and more dog toys. Training will also impact your budget, as will grooming expenses. And then there are those unexpected expenses. Perhaps your Yorkie will get into something sticky and the groomer will have to spend time trying to save his coat, or will have to shave him. Veterinary emergencies can be very expensive, especially if you need to take your dog in to an emergency after-hours clinic.

Before you make a commitment to a dog, make sure you'll have the financial ability to care for the dog throughout his lifetime. It's heartbreaking to love a dog yet not be able to care for him properly.

Even a Tiny Dog Takes Time

Taking care of a dog—even a tiny dog—takes time; more time than many people realize. Walking the dog, grooming him, cleaning up after him, playing with him, feeding him—even shopping for his food—takes time.

If you bring home a young puppy, you'll have to spend even more time with him as he will be afraid and lonely at first and your companionship will reassure him. Dogs from rescue or the shelter are usually older, but even older puppies or adult dogs will need time to get to know you and their new household.

Housetraining takes time, too, as does teaching the dog the household rules. Training takes time, both at home and at a training class. You'll also have to take the time to play with your dog, walk him, make sure he gets enough exercise, and socialize him.

Time with your dog is well spent; after all, most people get a dog for companionship, and that develops only when the two of you spend time together. Plus, dogs are social animals and are unhappy when left alone for long periods of time. However, if you live a very active life with many demands upon your time, think carefully about the time a dog will need before you bring one home.

A dog requires time and energy as well as money!

Got Energy to Spare?

People who own dogs quickly learn that they have acquired an additional shadow. A dog likes to be with you, watching everything you do, and interfering with what you're doing as much as possible. Puppies also like to get into stuff, chew up things, and raid the trash can. All healthy dogs like to play, and playing with you is much more fun than playing alone. Owning a dog takes a lot of energy, both to interact with the dog and to care for him.

Yorkie Smarts

Yorkies are active dogs from puppy-hood through old age! They love to hunt, chase, play, and explore. Can you keep up with one?

The Pros and Cons of Dog Ownership

In the past few years we have seen portrayals of numerous real life canine heroes. After the Oklahoma City bombing and World Trade Center and Pentagon disasters, canine search and rescue dogs worked day and night to find survivors. Therapy dogs comforted human searchers, survivors, and victims' families. We listened to the story of a World Trade Center survivor whose guide dog lead him safely from the doomed building. Canine heroes abound, and we honor them.

However, even canine heroes are dogs, and dog ownership has its pros and cons. My three dogs are certified therapy dogs and when working, they are awe-inspiring. However, at home, they are dogs just like any other. As with any relationship, there are good points and less than good points, so let's take a look at the pros and cons to owning a dog.

The pros:

- A dog will make you laugh, and laughter is always good for you.

- A dog will warn you of danger and so will increase your sense of security. Even a toy dog can do this for you.

- A dog will attract people's attention, enabling you to meet and talk to other people.

- A dog needs exercise and, by giving him that exercise, you'll get more, too.

- A dog needs to play, and play (along with laughter) is good for you, too.

- Research has shown that people who live with dogs are healthier than people who live alone.

- A dog is a great listener and wonderful therapy.

- A dog is a wonderful companion. You are never alone when you have a dog.

- A dog will love you unconditionally with all of his heart.

The cons:

- Dogs require a financial investment.

- Dogs can and often do make a mess. They can also be destructive.

- Dogs require your time and energy.

- You must be responsible; this life is dependent upon you.

- You must plan ahead and can't be as spontaneous when you have a dog.

- You will grieve when your dog grows old and dies.

The Pros Far Outweigh the Cons

I admit, I'm biased. I'm a dog owner, grew up with dogs, have always had dogs, and can't imagine life without dogs. As I write this, one dog is on my feet under the desk while another is asleep in the hall outside my office. My third dog is outside; I can hear her sniffing in the bushes outside my window.

Now, having three dogs requires quite a commitment. When my husband and I take a vacation we must plan ahead, and what we do must take the dogs into consideration. Because one of our dogs is older and has some health problems, even going out for dinner requires planning so that she can go outside to relieve herself on time. However, we both willingly do what is needed because our dogs add so much to our lives.

Watch Out!

The average cost of raising a puppy from eight weeks of age to one year is about $1,000, and that does not include the puppy's purchase price.

Not everyone is willing or able to do what we do, however. You need to look at your life and lifestyle and decide whether or not you can make a commitment to a dog. Can you do what the dog needs? Are you willing to do this for the next 14 to 16 years?

Yorkies are active dogs. Can you keep up?

A Yorkie's Unique Characteristics

Well, if you're still reading, you've probably decided that a dog would fit into your life and you're willing to commit to dog ownership. Congratulations! Now let's see whether a Yorkshire Terrier would really be the right dog for you or whether you would be better off with a less demanding dog.

The first thing you need to do is find a Yorkie—not to keep but just to get to know. Does a neighbor or friend have a Yorkie? You need to spend some time with the breed and get to know it. Seeing a Yorkie walking on the leash at the park isn't enough. Borrow your neighbor's Yorkie for the weekend; maybe your neighbor would like to go away for the weekend and you can pet sit for him. Get to know the dog, take him for walks, and play with him. See his activity level, his desire to play, and his watchfulness. Groom him so you know what his coat care will entail.

If you can get to know several Yorkies, that would be even better, as you could see a few dogs each with their own personalities. By getting to know several dogs, you'll have a better understanding of the breed.

Don't assume that just because you have owned dogs before and have read about Yorkies—even this book—that you don't need to get to know a Yorkie. Please don't skip this step! Yorkies are unique and not like most other breeds; even other terriers or other toys. Just ask any Yorkie owner!

Tiny Dogs

Yorkies are tiny. Usually between five to seven pounds when full grown, they are very small. Many people treasure this size, but it makes other people uneasy. A tiny dog can be severely hurt or killed if sat on or stepped on. Their size makes them more fragile and everything, including walks and playtimes, must be tailored to their size.

Always Affectionate

Yorkies are an affectionate breed. They are very loving, very demonstrative, and love to cuddle. Unfortunately, this can sometimes get out

of hand as some Yorkies spend their life on a lap, and they really do need to get down once in a while!

Bet You Didn't Know

Hunting is triggered by movement. If a cat sits still, the Yorkie may approach but will usually do so calmly and quietly. If the cat runs, however, the Yorkie will chase, usually while barking.

Tiny Hunters

Although they are tiny, Yorkies were originally hunting dogs and retain those instincts. A rat or a mouse (or a butterfly!) is not safe with a Yorkie chasing it! Yorkies can also chase and hunt cats, rabbits, hamsters, gerbils, or other small pets.

Protective and Courageous

It may seem ridiculous that a five- to seven-pound dog thinks he's a watchdog, but Yorkies do! Yorkies bark ferociously when someone approaches their yard, house, car, or person. They can't back up that bark with action, of course, but Yorkies don't seem to realize that. I guess they figure their barking will alert back-up, and it usually does.

Dog Talk

In conformation dog shows, dogs compete against others of their breed and winners accrue points towards their championship title.

Attitude Is Everything

Yorkies have a very regal attitude with their head held high, ears up, and coat flowing behind. If you can, go to a *conformation dog show* in your area and watch the Yorkies compete. Attitude is everything! This attitude is what earned them the name "King of Terriers."

Intelligent and Obedient

Yorkies are intelligent—very intelligent—and sometimes, too intelligent. Any dog trainer will tell you that Yorkies are smart, eager to learn, and easy to train. However, Yorkies are also smart enough to figure out alternative ways to do things, so training a Yorkie can also be a challenge! Yorkies are also smart enough to get bored, so training must be innovative and fun.

The Manipulative Yorkie

Okay, this is where Yorkies excel. Yorkies are very good at manipulating their owners. Those big dark eyes, gorgeous coat, tiny body, and wiggling tail stub can turn any owner into a puddle of mush. Yorkies know how cute they are and how well they are loved, and they use that to their advantage.

Pet Professionals Speak

My dog training business partner, Petra Gonzales, when asked how she would describe Yorkies said, "Most Yorkies are a ball of fire! They are reactive; they react before they think many times and they often bark while they do so." Many trainers commented on the breed's tendency to bark, both in excitement and as a watchdog.

Other trainers commented on the breed's excitability around children, sometimes to the point of snapping at kids. Tiny dogs are often not recommended for families with small children—the dogs are too small, too vulnerable, and often snap in retaliation. Many Yorkie breeders won't sell their puppies to families with young children.

A groomer, who asked not to be identified, said, "I wish they made mesh steel grooming gloves! Too many Yorkies are 'too cute' and spoiled rotten and too many try to take a bite out of me!" Another groomer said, "I wish people who get a long-coated breed

Yorkie Smarts

Although Yorkies are known for their long, flowing coats (often called show coats), many owners keep their Yorkies' coats clipped. Be sure you like the appearance both ways.

would either resign themselves to shaving it, or learn how to groom it properly. The dogs hate coming to the groomers because we have to untangle the mess the owners allowed to happen."

Don't Rush In!

Obviously, there are pros and cons to owning a dog, and to every breed. Some of the pros and cons also relate to you as a dog owner. To take just one example, if you keep a dog well groomed and free from tangles, the dog will be more comfortable and will be more relaxed with the groomer. If you let the dog get matted and take it to the groomer to have it combed out, the dog will have a difficult time and will probably act up for the groomer.

Don't rush into Yorkie ownership. Instead, get to know a Yorkie or two and think about the breed. Can you live with a dog like this? If you get a Yorkie and dislike an aspect of the breed, you can't change it! The breed is what it is. However, if you think that a tiny dog with these traits would suit you, well, congratulations!

The Least You Need to Know

- Take an objective look at your life and lifestyle and make sure dog ownership will be a good fit.
- Make sure you have the financial means to care for a dog.
- A dog will require a great deal of your time and energy.
- Get to know a Yorkie or two and make sure this is the right breed for you.

Chapter 2

What Is a Yorkshire Terrier?

In This Chapter

- 🏠 The history of Yorkies
- 🏠 Yorkies in the United States
- 🏠 The AKC Yorkshire Terrier standard
- 🏠 Yorkies today

Yorkshire Terriers attract attention everywhere they go, although many people can't identify the breed. Comments on their size, cuteness, and flowing coat are commonly followed by the question, "What kind of dog is this?" Some people confuse Yorkies with Silky Terriers, a similar but larger breed. Once people see a Yorkie, however, and learn what it is, they rarely forget!

Breed registries such as the American Kennel Club (AKC) publish what is called the breed standard for the more than 140 breeds recognized by the AKC. Created by the national breed clubs (in this case the Yorkshire Terrier Club of America), the AKC makes available the breed standard for each breed. The standard is a description of the ideal or "perfect" dog of that breed. At dog shows, judges compare each dog competing that day to the description of the perfect dog that is in the bred standard. The dog who comes closest to the standard is the winner. Breeders also use the standard to analyze potential breeding stock.

A breed is more than just its looks, however. A breed is also temperament and personality, its history and its purpose. So what makes Yorkies so unique? Let's see!

The History of the Breed

Small terriers of various kinds and varieties have been common in the British Isles for centuries. Other dogs, especially larger hunting dogs, could only be kept by landowners; the serfs could keep only small dogs. Landowners were afraid that with larger hunting dogs, the serfs would poach game on the landowners' property. So many serfs and other working people kept small terriers who would help control mice and rats.

During the Industrial Revolution, people whose families had worked the land for generations flocked to the factories and textile mills to try and better their lives. People from Scotland brought with them small dogs, some known as Clydesdale Terriers and others known as Paisley Terriers. Clydesdale Terriers weighed about 12 pounds and had a silky coat. The Paisley Terriers were about six pounds and were blue and tan.

It is known that these two breeds were crossed to produce a silky coated ratter; however, no pedigrees were kept, as most of the breeders were illiterate. Verbal histories, passed down through the generations, also spoke of crossings with English Black and Tan Terriers, Toy Terriers, and possibly even Maltese Terriers as well as other unnamed dogs of unknown breeds.

Eventually the dogs became more uniform in size, coat type, and color. In the mid-1880s, the dogs became known as Broken Haired Scottish Terriers. Then, in 1886, the British Kennel Club recognized these dogs as Yorkshire Terriers.

Dog Talk _____
Sire means father and **dam** means mother.

The Breed's Sire

Hudderfield Ben has been called the *sire* (or father) of the modern Yorkshire Terrier. Owned by M. A. Foster, Ben competed in conformation dog shows, winning frequently, and rat killing contests. Born in 1865, he was run over by a carriage in 1871, and died in the prime of life. However, his progeny went on to help establish the breed's popularity in England.

Bet You Didn't Know _____
Rat killing contests were popular in early England. A dog would be put in a pit with a number of rats, and the dog who killed the most rats in the shortest period of time was declared the winner. Since rats were a serious threat to human health, rat killing dogs were prized!

The Terrier Personality

The Yorkie's tough, "let me at'em" personality is a true terrier personality. Most of the small terriers were bred as ratters and had to have that personality. A small dog with a soft, sensitive temperament would not be as effective a ratter (rats are tough and can have a nasty bite!). Times were tough in that era, too, and often a family might not have enough food to go around. Many times the dog—who was fed table scraps anyway—might have to fend for himself. A hunting terrier could do that.

Popularity Soared!

After being recognized by the British Kennel Club, the breed's popularity increased, slowly at first, but increasing steadily. During the Victorian era, the wealthier ladies took to this attractive breed and kept it in increasing numbers. It was used as both a companion and as a ratter in the ladies' rooms.

In the early 1930s, fewer than 500 dogs were registered by the British Kennel Club, but by the mid-1950s more than 2,000 were registered. By the 1970s, the Yorkshire Terrier had become the most popular breed in England!

Today in England, the breed has reached a popularity level similar to its standing in the United States today, with registration figures showing it to be the seventh most popular breed in the country.

The Yorkie in the United States

The first recorded Yorkshire Terrier birth in the United States occurred in 1872. The breed was recognized by the AKC in 1885, and the first AKC Champion was Bradford Harry in 1889. A great-great-grandson of Hudderfield Ben, Harry was imported by P. H. Coombs.

Bet You Didn't Know

Yorkies were first shown at the Westminster Dog Show in 1878 with 18 in the over 5 pound class and 15 in the under 5 pound class.

The AKC Breed Standard

The AKC breed standard for the Yorkshire Terrier is the official written description of the ideal or perfect dog of this breed. Conformation dog show judges look at the dogs competing at each dog show, and compare those dogs to each other and to the standard to choose the best dog competing on that day.

Yorkies are black and tan as puppies and turn blue and tan as adults.

Yorkie breeders also use the standard as a guide to choose the best dogs for their breeding programs. The standard is what keeps a Yorkie looking like a Yorkie and not an Airedale!

The standard is broken down into several parts. Let's take a look at each part and then discuss it. Try to visualize each description in your mind as it is described, and fit the pieces together like a canine jigsaw puzzle.

> **General Appearance:** That of a long-haired toy terrier whose blue and tan coat is parted on the face and from the base of the skull to the end of the tail and hangs evenly and straight down each side of the body. The body is neat, compact and well proportioned. The dog's high head carriage and confident manner should give the appearance of vigor and self-importance.

Is attitude important? As the last sentence in this paragraph states, the writers of this standard certainly thought so. "Confident manner" and "self-importance" describe the Yorkie's mental attitude and personality. A Yorkie should not be timid, shy, fearful, or afraid.

The Yorkie's trademark coat is also mentioned here, as is the body shape, although both are mentioned in more detail in other sections.

Head: Small and rather flat on top, the skull not too prominent or round, the *muzzle* not too long, with the bite neither under shot nor overshot and teeth sound. Either scissors or level bite is acceptable. The nose is black. Eyes are medium in size and not too prominent; dark in color and sparkling with a sharp, intelligent expression. Eye rims are dark. Ears are small, V-shaped, carried erect and set not too far apart.

Dog Talk

Muzzle refers to the forward part of the skull from under the eyes forward that includes the nose, top and lower jaws, and the supporting bone.

This paragraph goes into great detail as to how the head should be shaped as well as details such as how the ears should be shaped and positioned. The dog's expression and intelligence are mentioned again; this time with the details of the eyes. Many toy breed dogs are known to have teeth problems but as this paragraph states, "The teeth should be sound." After all, a hunting terrier with bad teeth couldn't grasp and kill a rat!

Dog Talk

The **back line** is the view of the back from the side, looking at the back from the point of the shoulders to the hips, usually the base of the tail.

Body: Well proportioned and very compact. The back is rather short, the *back line* level, with the height at the shoulder the same as at the rump.

This is very plain and straightforward. The dog (under all that coat) should be small, tight and taut, and appear somewhat square with the ground, the dog's back, front legs, and back legs forming the sides of the square.

Legs and Feet: Forelegs should be straight, elbows neither in nor out. Hind legs straight when viewed from behind, but *stifles* are moderately bent when viewed from the sides. Feet are round with black toenails. *Dewclaws*, if any, are generally removed from the hind legs. Dewclaws on the front legs may be removed.

Dog Talk

The **stifle** is the joint of the back leg above the hock, which is the equivalent of the elbow of the back leg. **Dewclaws** are small toes and claws on the inside of the leg above the paw.

A hunting dog cannot function without strong legs and feet, and the Yorkie may be small but should still be thought of as a hunting dog. Nothing is to be exaggerated on this dog and he should remain an athlete with sound legs and feet.

Tail: Docked to a medium length and carried slightly higher than the level of the back.

In some parts of the world, tails may no longer be docked. In those situations, the tail is left natural with the coat parted on each side of the tail, making the tail a flag.

Coat: Quality, texture and quantity of coat are of prime importance. Hair is glossy, fine and silky in texture. Coat on the body is moderately long and perfectly straight (not wavy). Hair may be trimmed to floor length to give ease of movement and a neater appearance if desired. The fall on the head is long, tied with a bow in the center of the head or parted in the middle and tied with two bows. Hair on the muzzle is very long. Hair should be trimmed short on the tips of the ears and may be trimmed on the feet to give them a neat appearance.

Obviously, the coat is very important. Although the breed's attitude, personality, and size are important, the coat is what people see first. The coat also differentiates the Yorkie from other breeds. Therefore, great emphasis is placed upon it.

Colors: Puppies are born black and tan and are normally darker in body color, showing an intermingling of black hair in the tan until they have matured. Color of hair on the body and richness of tan on head and legs are of prime importance in adult dogs, to which the following color requirements apply: Blue: Is a dark steel-blue, not a silver-blue and not mingled with fawn, bronzy or black hairs. Tan: All tan hair is darker at the roots than in the middle, shading to still lighter tan at the tips. There should be no sooty or black hair intermingled with any of the tan.

Color on Body: The blue extends over the body from the back of the neck to root of tail. Hair on tail is a darker blue, especially at the end of the tail.

Bet You Didn't Know
Although the breed standard describes a long, flowing coat, many people shave or clip their Yorkies to reduce grooming time.

Bet You Didn't Know
Some histories seem to believe that the Yorkie at one time during its development weighed as much as 30 pounds. However, since most of the dogs used for its development were significantly smaller than that, it is highly unlikely the breed was ever that big.

Color on the Headfall: A rich, golden tan, deeper in color at the sides of the head, at ear roots and on the muzzle, ears a deep rich tan. Tan color should not extend down on back of neck.

Color on the Chest and Legs: A bright, rich tan, not extending above the elbow on the forelegs nor above the stifle on the hind legs.

As we can see by the preceding paragraphs, color is just as important as coat type and length in Yorkies. The specific blue and tan colors are explained quite well, as is the placement of those colors.

Weight: Must not exceed seven pounds.

By stating that dogs must not exceed seven pounds, the writers of this standard tried to ensure that this would remain a toy terrier; a very small dog.

Yorkies may be tiny but should still be athletic and strong for their size.

The British Kennel Club Standard

The Yorkie standard of the Kennel Club (KC) in Britain is very similar to the AKC standard. The general appearance is the same, with similar wording. However, there is a paragraph for both characteristics and temperament in which the Yorkie is described as an alert, intelligent toy terrier; spirited with an even disposition.

This standard also calls for a neck with "good reach," whereas the AKC standard doesn't mention the neck at all except to say that head should be carried high.

The KC standard also calls for a perfect scissors bite (the upper and lower teeth meet in a scissors motion) with teeth well placed. It calls for a complete bite, which normally means no missing teeth. As

Dog Talk

Movement is the dog's ability to gait (usually a trot) while the judge is watching. The dog's ability to move (or not) gives the judge clues as to the dog's physical conformation and athleticism.

we saw in the AKC standard, the AKC allows a scissors or level bite and there is no mention of a complete bite or missing teeth.

This standard also specifies the breed's gait or *movement* as "free with drive; straight action front and behind, retaining level topline" and the AKC standard does not mention gait at all.

Yorkies are very appealing to many people.

Using the Standard

Breed standards were written to keep a breed true to form and function. The Yorkie was bred to be a ratter, a vermin chaser, a tough, tenacious little dog. A ratter needs a strong body that is agile and moves well. The long coat actually had its purpose for those endeavors; it's difficult for a rat to bite a dog who has a flowing coat that disguises the body's outline under it. The Yorkie wasn't bred to be a lap dog, even though it is small enough to serve that purpose well.

Far too many of today's Yorkies are timid, shy, and fearful; and they should not be! A shy dog will never catch a mouse, never mind a rat! A fearful dog will never be a happy dog; to those dogs life is too scary! Breeders should keep temperament at the forefront when establishing a breeding program, and judges should not place a dog that obviously doesn't have the correct terrier temperament. Temperament and character are just as important as coat length and color.

Even though the vast majority of today's Yorkies will never hunt a rat, the breed's purpose must be kept in mind if the breed is to continue with the personality and character it is supposed to have.

The Yorkie Today

Yorkies have remained very popular, both in the dog show ring and as treasured pets. The Yorkie's attractive appearance is certainly appealing to many people, although numerous pet owners keep that high maintenance coat trimmed short or even shaved. The breed's tiny size is also a selling point for many people, but there are quite a few small toy breeds. However, when the breed's appearance and size are combined with the terrier temperament, well, that seems to create the perfect dog!

Yorkies today are also involved in many dog sports and activities. Although they cannot (because of their small size) compete in some sports, such as Frisbee catch, fetch, or weight-pulling contests, they can still have fun in many other activities, including the following:

🏠 **Agility.** This is a fast-moving, athletic sport where the dog jumps over jumps of different kinds, runs through tunnels, and climbs obstacles, all against a time clock.

🏠 **Conformation dog shows.** Dogs compete against others of their breed to win points toward a breed championship. Winners then compete against other breed winners for Best in Show. For conformation, the Yorkie must be kept in the long, flowing coat.

🏠 **Flyball.** A competitive relay race sport in which dogs run down a path, jump four hurdles, trigger a lever that throws out a tennis ball, and then return the way they came.

🏠 **Therapy Dog work.** Trained dogs who like people are evaluated and certified, and then visit people in nursing homes and hospitals as well as schools and day care centers.

🏠 **Freestyle.** In this sport, dogs and their owners dance to music using dance steps and obedience commands.

🏠 **Competitive Obedience.** Dogs and their owners work as a team, completing standard obedience exercises to earn titles.

Although not every dog is a show dog, Yorkie breeders have done a commendable job to keep the breed's appearance as close to the standard as possible. Most Yorkies are still athletes, too, and love to run, jump, and play. Too many Yorkies, however, don't show the bold, courageous temperament the breed should have. Hopefully breeders in the near future will take that into consideration. The breed deserves to carry its head high, as the standard says it should, and be bold and self-confident!

The Least You Need to Know

🏠 The Yorkie was developed as a ratter in England from Scottish and English Terriers.

🏠 The AKC standard describes the ideal Yorkie.

🏠 A Yorkie should always be more than just a lap dog; this is a tiny athlete well suited to many dog sports.

🏠 The Yorkie today should continue to be a bold, self-confident dog.

Chapter 3

The Yorkie Is a Terrier!

In This Chapter

- 🏠 Terriers are different!
- 🏠 The terrier personality says it all
- 🏠 A quick look at some popular terriers
- 🏠 The Yorkie in comparison

Terriers are very different from other dogs. Oh sure, they are canines, with the same genetic structure, but they are different in so many ways they might as well be a different species. There are physical differences—such as coat type—and there are a variety of temperament differences.

Recently, a woman enrolled in one of my basic obedience classes. She had a Jack Russell Terrier, a very popular breed right now, and was at her wit's end. "This dog is driving me to distraction!" she said, "She chews on everything and she will never relax!" I asked her, "Have you ever had a terrier before?" When she said no, I told her, "Welcome to the world of terrier ownership!" Terriers are different!

So that you can understand Yorkshire Terriers a little more before you bring one home, let's take a look at the world of terriers. We'll look at some of the more popular terriers right now, take a look at their personality characteristics, and then compare them to Yorkies. Let's make sure you are prepared for life with a terrier before you commit yourself!

Terriers Are Different

Golden Retriever owners expect their dogs to be social, affectionate, and calm. Labrador Retriever owners know that their dog will love to chase tennis balls, and German Shepherd owners understand that their dog will have the ability to be a good watch dog. What should terrier owners expect?

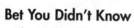

Bet You Didn't Know

The Yorkie (like the Silky Terrier) is a member of the toy group because of its size, but many people feel that the breed would be best represented in the terrier group because it is, and should remain, a true terrier.

Bet You Didn't Know

There are 26 breeds in the AKC terrier group. With two terriers in the toy group (Yorkshire Terriers and Silky Terriers) and three terriers in the Miscellaneous Group (Toy Fox Terrier, Glen of Imaal Terrier, and Black Russian Terrier) that makes a grand total of 31 AKC terrier breeds!

First of all, although the Yorkie is a member of the AKC toy group, let's take a look at the entire AKC terrier group.

The AKC terrier group consists of a variety of terriers, from the bigger Airedale to the smaller but look-a-like Welsh Terrier. All of the terriers were bred for a purpose; they all had a job to do. A great many of the terriers, including the Yorkie, were vermin hunters. Dogs who hunted vermin had to be agile, quick on their feet, tenacious, and stubborn. They had to think independently as they hunted on their own; no one was standing over them saying, "There's the rat behind that box—kill it now!" Although the terriers were companions, too, their hunting skills were vastly more important.

Terriers—including Yorkies—have attitude!

Alike but Different

Just as there are size, build, and coat differences between Golden
Retrievers, Labrador Retrievers, and Chesapeake Bay Retrievers,
terriers don't all have the same physical build or coat type.

Many terriers, including the Airedale, Welsh Terrier, Cairn Terrier,
and several others, have a coarse coat that is usually recognized as a
"terrier" coat. As we saw, though, the Yorkie has a long silky coat, as
does the Silky Terrier. The Soft-Coated Wheaten Terrier has, as its
name suggests, a very soft fine coat that is absolutely lovely.

However, all terriers—no matter what breed—are athletic. Some,
like the Skye Terrier, may have shorter legs than the Airedale or even
the smaller Welsh Terrier, but all are athletes in their own right.

Always on the Go!

Terriers are active, and the individual breeds don't make much difference as far as activity levels go, especially when compared to non-
terriers. Terriers are always ready to do something, go somewhere,
or chase something. A terrier's motto could easily be "Go, go, go!"

This activity level is great for people of the same temperament, but it can drive some people to distraction. Many terrier owners have asked me, "Why won't she just lie down and relax?" They just didn't realize when they brought home a terrier that this is a terrier trait.

Potential terrier owners should be active people.

The Terrier Personality

The terrier personality is what sets them apart so distinctly from other dogs. I asked several veterinarians, groomers, dog trainers, pet sitters, and even one gentleman who scoops dog feces in peoples' yards about their experiences with terriers. "How would you describe the average or typical terrier personality?" Most said terriers were feisty, independent, stubborn, single-minded, watchful, and potentially aggressive.

Many also used the term "reactive" to describe most terriers, with one veterinarian saying, "I have found that many terriers react first and think later." As a vermin hunter, that trait could be good; as a pet or as a patient at a veterinary clinic, that could be less desirable.

Several dog trainers said that terriers could be awesome in dog training classes when the dog was interested and wanted to cooperate. Their intelligence and stubbornness can make them wonderful students. However, if the dog was distracted by something else, their single-mindedness became a problem. One trainer said, "If the terrier's owner can find something that will motivate the dog—be it verbal praise, petting, dog treats, food, furry toys, or squeaky toys—the terrier will shine in training. However, if the dog is not to be motivated by the owner, well, then training can be difficult."

Terriers love a challenge. That challenge may be climbing a big hill, racing their owner to the dog toy in the backyard, or simply arguing. Many terrier owners say their dogs will refuse to cooperate with something—toenail trimming, brushing, training, or even something fun like going for a walk—just because refusing to do something is a good excuse for an argument.

In conformation dog shows, often judges will ask two terrier handlers to let their dogs face one another. Face to face the dogs will posture, try to look bigger or more aggressive than the other, or even bark at each other. This face-off, called *sparring*, is a way for the judge to see the terriers' attitude; the willingness to respond to a challenge and not back down.

Dog Talk

Sparring is when, in a conformation dog show class and at the judge's direction, two terriers are allowed to face each other and react, usually with posturing, to display their terrier attitude and personality.

Terriers and Other Dogs

Terriers aren't always particularly good with strange dogs, although they live well with other dogs in the household. With their feisty attitudes, terriers will often instigate trouble with strange dogs, even when the other dog is much larger.

My dogs and I routinely see a West Highland White Terrier on our morning walks. This terrier is quite old, obviously arthritic, and walks very slowly. However, when my three dogs and I walk past, he lunges to the end of his leash, barks, snarls, and acts like he is personally going to rip up all three! Once we are past, he stops, breathes heavily, and continues his slow walk.

Terriers and Other Pets

Terriers are not to be trusted alone with small animals, including other household pets. Because they are hunters, pets such as hamsters, gerbils, rabbits, and even cats can be viewed as potential prey. Whereas many other dogs may chase the household cat but wouldn't hurt it, terriers have been known to chase and kill cats and other small animals.

Most terrier breeders, when placing a terrier in a home, advise against keeping other small pets, or caution the owners to make sure the other pets are kept out of the terrier's reach at all times.

Some Popular Terriers

Now that we've seen what terriers are like as a group, let's take a look at some specific breeds and compare them to Yorkshire Terriers. Hopefully this comparison will confirm for you that Yorkies are the right breed for you, or let you know that Yorkies (and perhaps terriers in general) are not the right breed for you before you have committed yourself to the breed.

We'll start with the breeds most like the Yorkie in one way or another. Please keep in mind these are breed traits as described by a variety of pet professionals who routinely see a variety of terriers. There will be exceptions, though; every dog is an individual, and there will be certain dogs in each breed who may or may not fit these descriptions.

Silky Terriers

Silky Terriers look more like Yorkies than any other breed. Silkies have, as the name suggests, a long silky blue and tan coat. Although enthusiasts of each breed will quickly point out the differences in the coats, they are actually very similar. The Silky is about nine pounds in weight while the Yorkies should be no larger than seven pounds.

Both breeds are affectionate and devoted to their owners. The Silky is a reactive breed, but no more so than the Yorkie. Both are watchful and protective of the home, and both can have a tendency to bark. Dog trainers argue over which is more open to training; some say the Silky is, while others argue for the Yorkie. Both can be snappy toward young children and neither should be trusted with small animals.

Cairn Terriers

Cairn Terriers are hunters with a strong prey drive, stronger than seen in today's Yorkies. Cairns are a small, sturdy, normally buff-colored terrier. Toto in the *Wizard of Oz* was a Cairn Terrier. Cairns are reactive, active, playful, and inquisitive. They tend to be barkers; sometimes even more than Yorkies. Cairns are more destructive and more watchful than Yorkies but less than Westies.

Cairn Terriers are more people-oriented than many other terriers but are not any more so than Yorkies. Cairns are normally better with children (less apt to snap) than Yorkies. Cairns accept training as well as Yorkies do; better than most other terriers. Cairns are usually easier to housetrain than Yorkies.

West Highland White Terriers

Westies have a very different coat than Yorkies; a coarser more terrier-like coat. Westies are larger than Yorkies—a medium sized terrier—and are quite sturdy. In temperament, both breeds are quite reactive, watchful, and protective, and both have a tendency to bark. Westies, however, are usually more aggressive than Yorkies, both toward people as well as other dogs and other animals.

Westies are loyal to family and home but are not as demonstrative as are Yorkies and Silkies. Westies have a tendency to be more destructive, especially as puppies, while Yorkies are harder to housetrain. Yorkies are easier to obedience train than Westies.

Scottish Terrier

Scotties can be quite reactive, although not normally as reactive as Yorkies and Westies. A medium-size terrier, larger than Yorkies and about the same size as Westies, Scotties are strong and tough. Like Westies, Scotties are very watchful and can be quite aggressive and protective. Scotties have a very dominant personality, more so than does the Yorkie, although Yorkies are no slouches in that regard!

Scotties are very loyal dogs. Although family and home are important, they are not as demonstrative as Yorkies. Scotties can be challenging to train, more so than Yorkies, although they do better in training than Westies. Scotties are easier to housetrain than Yorkies.

Fox Terriers

Fox Terriers are taller than Yorkies, with a short coat, and are very athletic. They are very reactive, much more so than Yorkies. They are also known to be barkers, and many can become nuisance barkers. Fox Terriers are watchful and protective; much like the Yorkie. Fox Terriers enjoy a challenge, much more so than Yorkies; can be even more destructive than Westies; and can be quite difficult to housetrain.

Yorkies and Westies share many terrier traits yet are still very different breeds.

Fox Terriers love their family, although they can be snappy toward children and are known for trying to assert dominance over the household. Training is necessary although it is usually a challenge—much more so than with Yorkies.

Jack Russell Terriers

Jack Russell Terriers are very similar to Fox Terriers. They vary in size but almost all are larger than Yorkies. They can have a short coat or a wire haired coat. They are very reactive, can be potential problem barkers, are watchful and protective; all more so than Yorkies. They are usually easier to housetrain than Fox Terriers but can be just as destructive.

Jack Russell Terriers don't always show their affection for their family, although family is important to them. They try to dominate their family much more than Yorkies do. Training is always needed for Jack Russells and is always a challenge.

Is a Terrier—Including a Yorkie—Right for You?

One terrier owner told me, "Owning a terrier is not just owning a dog; it's a lifestyle!" Although she didn't want to be identified for her profound statement, it's very true. Sharing your life with a terrier is not like owning any other dog; life with a terrier is never boring!

Before adding any terrier to your family—including a Yorkie—make sure you'll be comfortable and happy with the changes in your life. As we saw, terriers are pushy, assertive, reactive, and challenging. Those characteristics are horrible to someone who has chosen Golden Retrievers or German Shepherds as their breed of choice, but those same characteristics can bring smiles to the faces of people who enjoy challenges.

A friend of mine, Kerry Siekmann of Carlsbad, California, adopted a Jack Russell Terrier with behavior problems. A dog trainer, she knew exactly what she was in for but laughed and did it anyway! Barbee hands her a challenge on a daily basis but Kerry loves it! "Barbee makes me smile," she said, "And none of these behaviors are directed at me personally. This is just who she is." Kerry figures she will still be obedience training Barbee when the dog dies of old age, and the thought of that doesn't bother her one little bit.

The Least You Need to Know

- The personality of terriers is very different from most other breeds.
- All terrier breeds share some characteristics but in varying degrees.
- Before you bring home any terrier, make sure you will be comfortable with the changes that will come with it.
- Sharing your life with a terrier is more than owning a dog; it's a lifestyle!

4

Finding a Yorkie for You

In This Chapter

- 🏠 Finding a reputable breeder
- 🏠 Considering rescued dogs
- 🏠 Other ways to find a dog
- 🏠 Choosing the right Yorkie for you

So far we've considered the responsibilities of owning a dog, and you've looked at yourself, your daily routine, and your budget to see if dog ownership is right for you. And then we've looked at Yorkies specifically, and in comparison to other terriers, to see whether Yorkie ownership is a realistic choice for you. If you're still committed to getting a Yorkie, the next step is to find that one special Yorkshire Terrier who is just right for you.

We'll take a look at breeders first and explain what will happen when you contact a breeder. Yorkie rescue is also a way to find a special dog, and the Yorkie rescue network does a great job finding homes for homeless dogs. People can also acquire dogs from other sources, including their local animal shelters, and we'll discuss the pros and cons of doing that.

We'll also go through the process of choosing the right dog for you. Each individual dog has his own personality traits that make him unique, and those traits could be perfect for you or horrible. We'll show you how to choose that special dog whose personality will complement your own.

Finding a Reputable Breeder

The best place to find your Yorkie is from a reputable breeder. What makes a breeder "reputable"?

- A reputable breeder chooses her breeding stock carefully, using the breed standard as a guide to try and produce the best puppies she can.

- A reputable breeder uses health tests to try and eliminate any unhealthy dogs from her breeding program.

- A reputable breeder listens to the owners of dogs from her breeding program to hear the good and the bad points of her dogs.

- A reputable breeder will supply buyers with proof of health screening, a sales contract, and references.

- A reputable breeder knows that Yorkies are not the right breed for everyone and screens potential buyers so she can weed out those who wouldn't be happy with her dogs.

- A reputable breeder will always take back a dog from her breeding program that can no longer remain in its home.

- A reputable breeder loves her breed and continues to educate herself so that her dogs continue to improve.

Breeders look for responsible homes for their puppies.

Finding That Special Breeder

There are lots of ways to find a special breeder. You can go to a local dog show and watch the Yorkies compete. When they are through competing, talk to some of the people showing. Ask to meet their dogs and ask about their breeding programs or where they got their dogs. The American Kennel Club can also give you a referral to a breeder's list.

If someone in your neighborhood has a nice Yorkie, ask where they got him and find out if the

Yorkie Smarts

The Yorkshire Terrier Club of America can be reached at www.ytca.org or at Yorkshire Terrier Club of America, Secretary, PO Box 271, St. Peters, PA 19470-0271.

owner would recommend doing business with that breeder. Your veterinarian might also know of a local breeder who takes good care of her dogs.

What Is a Backyard Breeder?

A *backyard breeder* is someone who breeds their dogs but doesn't usually do as much research as is needed to do it well. Sometimes a backyard breeder will breed once or twice and stop—finding it more difficult than they realized—or this person may breed every year, hoping to make some money from her dogs.

A backyard breeder may produce a nice dog, but when that happens, it's usually an accident. Most often a backyard breeder has no way of knowing what kind of dogs she will produce because she doesn't fully understand the process.

Dog Talk

A **backyard breeder** is someone who has bred her dog but does not have the knowledge about dogs and her breed that a reputable breeder has worked so hard to learn.

The best thing a backyard breeder can do is to ask for help from a reputable breeder. If a seasoned, knowledgeable breeder will mentor her, she can then improve the quality of her dogs and will no longer be referred to as a backyard breeder.

Dog Talk

Puppy mills are commercial operations that produce puppies in large numbers. Dogs are kept in cages and no screening is done as to health, temperament, or working ability.

What Is a Puppy Mill?

A *puppy mill* is a breeder who produces puppies strictly as a commodity and doesn't care for the emotional and physical well-being of his dogs. Often a puppy mill is a farm, with dogs in cages. Sometimes a puppy mill is a private residence with far too many dogs. In any case, the dogs being used to produce the puppies are not cared for properly, are usually bred each season with no recuperation, and the puppies are taken from their mother much too early so that they can arrive in pet stores at eight weeks of age. Puppy mill breeders don't screen the breeding dogs for health problems, either, nor do they choose dogs with the best temperaments for breeding.

Yorkie Smarts

Yorkies are, unfortunately, found in puppy mills. One was broken up in Valley Center, California, where many Yorkies were filthy, ungroomed, with infected eyes, tangled coats, sore feet from the wire cages, and full of fleas and ticks. The tiny Yorkie puppies were unsocialized, and numerous dogs had to be euthanized.

Questions to Ask

When you find a breeder you would feel comfortable doing business with, ask her some questions. She will be expecting this, so don't be embarrassed.

🏠 **How long have you been breeding?** Some experience is better, however, a gazillion years experience isn't always best, either. Sometimes the "old timers" never allow themselves to learn anything new.

🏠 **What health problems do you screen your dogs for?** If she says her dogs don't have any health problems, run the other way—fast! Although Yorkies are, for the most part, healthy, they are prone to some problems, so make sure the breeder is being honest with you.

🏠 **What kind of guarantee do you offer with your dogs?** Is the dog guaranteed free of hereditary health defects? This is very important to you. I have an eight-year-old dog who is suffering from a congenital (inherited) liver problem. We love her dearly but her health care and medication runs us over $150 a month. That's expensive, and her breeder isn't helping us nor did he give us any satisfaction once she was diagnosed. Obviously, we will not be going back to that breeder.

🏠 **Can I stop by to see some of your dogs?** The answer must be yes, even if the breeder has no puppies at the moment. Seeing several dogs will give you an idea of what her breeding program produces.

Watch Out!

The breeder shouldn't take offense when you ask her questions about her dogs and her breeding program.

🏠 **Do you belong to any dog organizations?** Membership in Yorkshire Terrier clubs or organizations can help breeders continue their education in the breed. New information in veterinary medicine and other vital information is shared with members.

When You Visit the Breeder

When you visit the breeder for the first time, look for a few things:

🏠 Is her place clean? Feces should be picked up and urine puddles cleaned up. Hopefully, the dogs are in the house and house-trained.

🏠 Are the dogs well-groomed? Yorkies require coat care, and they should not be tangled or matted. However, don't fault her if they are shaved or have haircuts. Many breeders keep their show dogs in long coat but clip the others just for ease of care.

🏠 Are the dogs bright-eyed, alert, and healthy? A dog who doesn't feel good should be isolated from the other dogs. If several dogs are droopy, sneezing, or coughing, go elsewhere.

🏠 Does the breeder call each dog by name, and does the dog respond? Sometimes breeders get overwhelmed and have too many dogs. She should know each dog by sight, and each dog should know his or her name and come when called.

If the breeder has puppies, she should be able to show you the registration papers for that litter as well as pedigrees. Her paperwork must be in order or you won't be able to register your puppy. The breeder should also show you a copy of her sales contract; make sure you read it and understand it completely.

Watch Out! _____

Registration papers from the AKC or other registries are not an assurance of quality. They simply mean the parents of the litter were registered.

Ask the breeder for some references, too, and then later, follow through and call these people. Were they happy with their puppy? Would they do business with this breeder again? Is their puppy healthy? If there was a problem, was it resolved to their satisfaction? Don't hesitate to ask questions, as this is an important part of the screening process.

Expect Questions

Reputable breeders are protective of their dogs; they don't want their dogs to end up in the wrong home, in local animal shelters, or in rescue programs. Reputable breeders ask as many questions of potential buyers as buyers should ask breeders. You'll want information about the breeder's dogs but the breeder wants to make sure you can give one of her dogs the best home possible!

Some of the questions the breeder may ask you include the following:

- 🐾 **Have you owned a dog before?** If so, did it live out its life with you? The breeder wants to make sure you are committed to caring for your dogs, including her puppy, should she sell you one.

- 🐾 **How much do you know about Yorkies?** She is going to want to make sure you know what you're getting into! Terriers, even Yorkies, are not for everyone.

- ⌂ **Do you have small children?** Very few Yorkie breeders will sell a puppy (or even an adult) to a family with small children. Yorkies are tiny, fragile, and not the best playmates for kids. In addition, if a Yorkie feels threatened, he may snap, and snapping at kids is not good!

- ⌂ **Is your backyard securely fenced in?** The breeder wants to make sure your yard is safe for a tiny puppy and dog.

Expect other questions, too, and don't be offended if she asks about your family, your home, or even your finances. She is simply being protective of her puppies.

You should be comfortable taking a puppy home from this breeder.

Take a Look at Yorkie Rescue

Purebred dog rescue has become very popular in the past decade as the numbers of purebred dogs being euthanized in shelters has grown. Enthusiasts of purebred dogs were horrified to find dogs of their breed being killed when potential adopters could be found. Rescue groups were formed to help save individual breeds. Some rescue groups are sponsored by national and regional breed clubs, while other groups operate independently of clubs.

The primary Yorkshire Terrier rescue group is Yorkshire Terrier National Rescue, Inc. (YTNR). This group was founded in 1997 and is dedicated to saving Yorkies. The group saves dogs from shelters, screens potential adopters, and does follow up visits after the adoption. All dogs are spayed and neutered, vaccinations are updated, and dogs are microchipped for identification. Information on YTNR is available on the Internet at www.yorkierescue.com.

The Rescue Process

You can find a rescue group in your area by contacting a national group and asking if there is a local point of contact, or by checking with your local shelter or animal control. They normally keep a list of local breed rescue groups.

Most groups will ask you to fill out an application and, when that is received, will conduct an interview. Some of the interviews may be by e-mail, phone, at the rescue group's office, or at your home. When you're approved for an adoption, you'll either be placed on a waiting list or will be told of any dogs who are available. The procedures followed by different rescue groups vary; sometimes a volunteer will want to see your home and yard while others will interview you over the telephone.

Although you won't be able to get as much information about the dog from rescue as you would from a breeder, you can usually find out if the dog is healthy, if he's housetrained, and how he accepts grooming—three very important things!

When you and a dog hit it off, you'll make an application to adopt that dog. Most rescue groups do at least one follow up visit (if not more) to make sure the dog is settling in okay and that you have things under control. The rescue groups don't want to see their dogs back in rescue again, so they take every care to make sure the adoption is going to work out.

Bet You Didn't Know

Dogs end up in rescue for horrible reasons. A four-year-old Yorkie, unneutered male, was turned in because he wasn't housetrained, yet the owner had never called a trainer for help. A lovely adult female was turned in because her owner redecorated and the dog no longer matched!

Other Ways to Find a Dog

There are several other ways to find a dog. Although you can usually get a better dog with a known history from a breeder, some people like the feeling of saving a dog's life and therefore prefer to get a dog who would otherwise be euthanized. Other people prefer to get a dog directly from its first owner and that, too, is fine. There are many different ways to find a dog.

Shelter Dogs

Many shelter dogs are absolutely wonderful companions.

Adopting a dog from a shelter can warm your heart; there can be a sense of pleasure involved with saving a life. However, the down side to shelter adoptions is that you'll be getting an unknown. You won't know this dog's health history or ancestry. You won't know whether the dog has had any training or even if the dog is housetrained.

However, you can still ask questions. Ask the shelter staff what they have noticed about the dog. Is she clean in her run? Does she bark a lot? Does she walk nicely on a leash? How does she accept grooming? Was any information given about her when she was turned in?

Privacy laws in many states forbid the shelters from giving you many details, but sometimes you can piece together information by simply asking questions in a way that the staff can answer them. Find out as much as you can before you decide to bring home a dog from the shelter.

Private Party Adoptions

Dogs are given up by their owners for awful reasons—such as not matching the décor—but sometimes an owner simply cannot keep a dog. Perhaps an elderly owner lost his spouse and now must go to a nursing home. In military neighborhoods, the marine, sailor, or soldier may get orders overseas. There are times when well-loved pets need new homes.

In these situations, don't get caught up in the emotions of the moment. You're still looking for the right dog for you, so ask many of the same questions you would ask a breeder. If you get a bad feeling or have reservations, don't take the dog and certainly don't let anyone make you feel guilty for not taking him.

If you're considering taking the dog, try to spend some time with him. Play with him, run a comb through his coat, and if you can, take him for a walk. See if his personality shows, and pay attention to any behavior problems he might have. Make sure you'll be comfortable with this dog should you decide to take him.

Pet Stores

Reputable breeders don't sell their puppies to pet stores. Reputable breeders want to know who is buying their puppies and that they will be well cared for. Therefore, the sources of puppies in pet stores are usually questionable. Some may come from backyard breeders, but most come from puppy mills.

Choosing the Right Dog for You

There is less variety in Yorkie temperaments than there is in many other breeds; however, some Yorkies are bolder than others, shyer than others, or more stubborn. So even though you have decided that a Yorkie is the right breed for you, you still need to choose the individual dog with a personality that will mesh with yours.

Your Own Personality

Be honest about your own personality. Are you quiet and intro- verted? Boisterous and extroverted? Or somewhere in between? Are you bossy? Do you like to have your own way? Or do you prefer to give in so there isn't a fuss? When choosing a puppy, try to choose one with a personality that will not conflict with your own.

If you are …

- **Quiet, shy, introverted.** Choose a puppy or dog who is also quiet, but don't choose a shy dog. If both of you are shy, you will reinforce that trait. Instead, choose a dog who is quiet but also outgoing and self-confident.

- **Compliant.** Choose a Yorkie who is calm but not bold. A bold terrier would take advantage of you.

- **Boisterous, bossy, and extroverted.** Take the boldest puppy in the litter; you two will have a blast together!

Boys or Girls?

Both male and female Yorkies can be great friends and companions, but each sex does have some unique characteristics. The thing to keep in mind is that to be a good pet, neither sex needs adult sexual hormones, so the males should be neutered and the females spayed.

Neutered males are usually quite sweet. They can be great fun and quite rowdy, depending upon their individual personalities, but for the most part, they are loving and affectionate. Spayed females are affectionate, too, but they can also be a bit bossy.

As a general rule, I suggest male dogs for female dog owners and female dogs for male dog owners. This seems to work well with fewer conflicts.

Bet You Didn't Know

If you already have a dog, make your new dog one of the opposite sex. There are fewer disagreements when you keep a spayed or neutered dog of either sex than when you keep two dogs of the same sex.

Talk to the Breeder

Yorkie litters are often very small—two to three puppies is normal. Very rarely there may be five to six puppies. So in any given litter, you might not have much choice when looking for the right puppy.

The breeder has been watching this litter since they were born and knows the puppies well. If you tell her about yourself, your likes and dislikes, your daily routine, activity level, and what you're look-ing for in a puppy, let her then guide you in choosing the right puppy. She knows which puppy is the boldest and the first to do things. She also knows which puppy hangs back and lets his sister or brother blaze the way.

When the breeder suggests a puppy, get to know that puppy. If the breeder will allow you, come and visit with the puppy a few times. Watch the puppy with its littermates and watch it alone. Interact with the puppy as much as the breeder and mother dog will allow.

Then, when you know that this is the right puppy for you, go ahead and make that commitment.

Listen to Your Heart

Choosing the right puppy or dog can be hard. An emotional decision is rarely the right one, yet the decision cannot be made totally without emotion. Be logical and think about your decision, and when your brain tells you it's right, then let your heart guide you.

My youngest dog was not a planned decision. I was at a dog event when his breeder walked up to me and placed an eight-week-old puppy in my arms. She said, "I know you loved his grandmother. Well, she has passed away and this is the last litter from his mom. Do you want him?" How could I say no to a small black and tan puppy licking my face?

In this case, I knew the breeder and knew the puppy's ancestors, so I really didn't need to do any research. However, because I wasn't planning on getting a puppy at that time, it was simply an emotional decision. Of course, I took him home!

The Least You Need to Know

- A reputable breeder will be able to answer all your questions, so don't be shy; ask!
- Adopting a dog from Yorkie rescue is something to consider, although you may not know much about the dog.
- Adopting a Yorkie from a shelter will save his life, but you won't know anything about him.
- Don't take home just any Yorkie; choose the right dog for you.

Part  There's a Puppy in the House!

A Yorkie puppy is so cute! This tiny, fluffy, black and tan mite is so adorable—and so very, very smart! So to prevent future disasters, let's get started on the right foot.

The very first thing you need to do, even before bringing home your new puppy, is to make sure you're ready for him. That means puppy-proofing the house and yard to make sure he'll be safe. You'll also need to go shopping for some basic supplies.

Once your puppy is home, you'll need to begin teaching him some basic household rules. Keep a vision in your mind of what you want this dog to be like when he grows up, and train him with that vision in mind; otherwise, this smart little puppy will train you!

Puppyhood is a busy but important time, so keep reading.

Chapter 5

Prior Planning Is Everything!

In This Chapter

- 🏠 Puppy-proofing your house
- 🏠 Puppy-proofing your yard
- 🏠 Getting help from pet professionals
- 🏠 A checklist of supplies

Once your new Yorkie joins your family, life will never be the same. It's amazing how much difference that tiny bit of life can make. But don't worry about all that change; it's all definitely for the better!

Before you bring home your new best friend, you'll want to take a good hard look at your house and yard and make sure they are safe. A tiny Yorkie puppy can get into much more mischief than you might guess, so we'll talk you through the puppy-proofing process!

You'll also want to talk with some pet professionals. Your veterinarian will be especially helpful in assisting you to maintain your

Yorkie's good health, and a groomer will teach you all about that luscious coat and how to care for it. You'll also want to start your Yorkie in puppy class soon, so find a trainer you trust.

You may also need to go shopping prior to bringing home your puppy. We'll go through a checklist and see what you'll need.

Puppy-Proofing Your House

One of the biggest mistakes many puppy owners make is giving their young puppy too much freedom. Young puppies don't realize that chewing on an electrical cord can shock and kill them; they just see this thing dangling in front of their nose that looks like it would be fun to chew on. Because puppies have no common sense and need constant supervision, you need to limit your puppy's freedom and make sure the rooms where he is allowed are safe. We'll talk about limiting his freedom more in this and the next chapter, but first let's talk about how to make your house safe.

In the rooms where you'll allow the puppy to run around (under your supervision, of course) get down on your hands and knees and look at things from a puppy's point of view. Are there magazines that could be chewed up? Pick them up and put them away. Books on the bottom bookshelf? Those are fun to chew. Cords dangling from behind the television, DVD player, and stereo? Remote controls on the sofa end table? Go through the rooms and put away everything valuable, chewable, or dangerous that is within reach.

Watch Out!

Don't assume a puppy will not or cannot chew up something. Puppies are tenacious and stubborn when they want something.

Here are some things that puppies commonly chew on:

🏠 Electrical cords

🏠 Telephone cords

- Remote controls
- Cell phones
- Books and magazines
- Food, dishes, cups, and utensils
- Shoes and socks
- Children's toys
- Medicine bottles

Yorkie Smarts

If you think your Yorkie has eaten something potentially poisonous, the National Poison Control Hotline is 1-800-222-1222 or the ASPCA Animal Poison Control number is 1-888-426-4435.

Before your puppy comes home, have everyone in the house get into the habit of putting things away, picking stuff up, and closing bedroom or closet doors. When it becomes a habit to do these things, the house becomes much safer for the puppy. Make sure, too, everyone understands the new rules. If someone leaves their slippers in the room on the floor and they get chewed up, it's not the puppy's fault. He doesn't know any better until he's been taught the rules.

Dangerous Stuff

Keeping your dog safe means he'll be around longer for you to love and for him to love you. Our homes are full of dangerous things. Make sure all of these things are put away and safely out of your puppy's reach.

Some dangerous stuff:

- **Around the house.** Cigarettes (and their ashes and butts), pens and felt tip pens, many different houseplants, laundry products, hobby supplies, and potted plants.
- **In the kitchen.** Oven cleaners, floor cleaners and wax, bug spray, insect traps, furniture polish, and dishwasher soaps and rinses.

🏠 **In the bathroom.** Medicines, vitamins, bathroom cleaners, toilet bowl cleaners, some shampoos and conditioners, hair coloring products, and many makeup items. Don't forget the toilet scrub brush.

Watch Out!

Don't assume your Yorkie will avoid dangerous substances. Instead, assume he will get into them and make sure they're out of reach!

🏠 **In the garage and yard.** Car maintenance products, including oils, gas, and antifreeze; fertilizers; weed and insect control products; snail and slug bait; mouse and rat traps and baits; and paints and paint removers. If you have a pool, many of the treatment products are also dangerous. Some landscaping plants are poisonous.

Limit Freedom

One of the easiest ways to help protect your Yorkie is to limit his freedom. Use baby gates to restrict him to one room at a time—preferably the room you're in, also—so you can watch him. When you can't watch him, put him in his kennel crate (we'll talk about that more later) or put him in a child's playpen or exercise pen. An exercise pen is a heavy wire fence that works just like a child's playpen; it keeps the puppy confined but gives him enough room to play.

By limiting his freedom, you can protect him from harm and keep him safe while at the same time prevent him from learning bad habits.

In addition, tiny Yorkie puppies can get into very small spaces. Yorkies can fit beside and behind the refrigerator, under the dishwasher, under the foot of the reclining chair, through a tiny hole in the screen door, and many other dangerous places. When puppy-proofing your house, think small—if a kitten can fit through it, so can a Yorkie!

Puppy-Proofing Your Yard

You need to puppy-proof your yard just as you did your house. Make sure the kids' toys are put away, the gardening supplies are out of reach, all poisonous plants are out of reach (see list later in this chapter), and the pool chemicals are stored in a safe place. Assume that if anything is left within reach, the puppy will chew on it.

Look at the yard from your puppy's point of view. Can he get under the deck, and is it dangerous if he does? Is there a place where he can get through the vent under the house? Can he chew on the cords to the lights in the backyard? Does the television cable go into the house inside the yard? Can the puppy chew on those cables? There are many things in the backyard that are potentially danger-ous or that the puppy can destroy.

Inspect the Fence

Terriers, including Yorkies, are curious. If there's a hole in the fence around your yard, your Yorkie will stick his nose in it. If he can make the hole bigger, he will. He may not want to actually go any-where, he's just curious about what's on the other side of the fence.

Make sure the fence itself is sound and all holes—even tiny ones—are covered. It may be a good idea to run hardware cloth (wire fencing) over the inside of the fence, from tight to the ground to about three feet high.

Make sure there are no holes under the fence, either. If there is a gap between the ground and the fence, a tiny Yorkie can dig enough to get under it.

Bet You Didn't Know

If you think your fence won't be secure or that your yard has too many dangers, build your Yorkie a dog run. A fenced area that's 4 feet wide by 12 feet long is more than enough.

Dangerous Plants

Many common landscaping plants are dangerous. Some will just make a dog nauseous, but others are toxic. Before allowing your puppy free access to the yard, make sure none of these plants are present.

The plants in the following list are some of the most commonly used landscaping plants that are dangerous for pets; however, if you have any doubts about any plants in your yard or garden, talk to a horticulturist or a poison control center. As the saying goes, "It's always better to be safe than sorry!"

Amaryllis

Avocado (leaves not fruit)

Azalea

Belladonna

Bird of paradise

Bottlebrush

Boxwood

Buttercup

Calla lily

Common privet

Crocus

Daffodil

Dieffenbachia

Dogwood

English ivy

Foxglove

Hemlock

Horse chestnut

Hyacinth

Iris

Jasmine

Lily of the valley

Milkweed

Morning glory

Mushrooms

Oleander

Pennyroyal

Poison ivy, oak, and sumac

Rhododendron

Sweet pea

Tulip

Yew

Is your yard safe for a tiny puppy?

Pet Professionals Can Help

Dog owners do not—and should not—try to cope with dog ownership alone. Why suffer through bad behavior when a trainer can
help you do things with much less hassle? Why teach your Yorkie to
hate it when you brush through those tangles when a groomer can
show you an easier way? Let professionals help you; that's why they
do what they do!

You can find pet professionals in your area in several different
ways, but the most reliable is usually by personal referrals. If you ask
several dog owners which veterinarian they recommend, and one
name keeps popping up, well, he or she would be a good choice.

Watch Out!

Don't wait until an emergency to find pet professionals. Do your research before you need help.

Yellow page ads are fine; coupons in the mail are okay, but keep in mind anyone can place an ad. However, people who have done business with pet professionals can tell you about firsthand experiences.

Make an Appointment

When you have a few referrals to some pet professionals, call and make an appointment to meet with each one. They may or may not ask for you to pay for their time, but if they do, please remember their time is their money! When you meet with them, ask a few questions:

- What are their business hours?

- What is the business telephone number?

- What are their payment procedures? Do they have any financing for emergencies (especially the veterinarian) or do they accept credit cards? Which ones?

- Are they familiar with Yorkies?

- Are the veterinarians familiar with health problems Yorkies might face?

- Is the groomer comfortable working with the Yorkie coat? What does she think about clipping or shaving a Yorkie, if you decide to do that?

- Does the trainer understand the housetraining difficulties faced by toy breed dogs? Does she like working with terriers? Does she have any tricks up her sleeve to help toy breed owners?

Once you decide which pet professionals you feel most comfortable with, set up a client chart with them. Then, once your Yorkie comes home, you can begin business with them as needed.

A Supply Checklist

Okay, so your house is puppy-proofed and your yard is safe for a puppy (or you have set up a dog run). You have found a few pet professionals you feel comfortable with, and you have a Yorkie on the way. What else do you need? How about some dog food? Food and water bowls? A leash and collar? Your Yorkie is going to need some supplies, so let's make a list!

Dog Run

We talked about a dog run briefly earlier in this chapter. Yorkies are tiny dogs and can get through some amazingly small holes in a fence. If you have any doubts whatsoever as to whether your Yorkie will be safe in your backyard, build him a dog run. It doesn't have to be huge—a 12 feet long by 4 feet wide run will be fine for your Yorkie for his entire life. Just make it escape proof, with no gaps between the ground and the bottom of the fence, and if you live in an area with birds of prey (hawks or eagles) make sure the run has fencing over the top.

Watch Out!
Birds of prey—including hawks and eagles—have been known to pick up, fly off with, and consume tiny dogs. Never leave a Yorkie out in the backyard unattended if you live in an area where birds of prey hunt.

Food and Water Bowls

You'll want two bowls with relatively shallow sides. Yorkie puppies are not tall, and even some cereal bowls will be too tall for them. Ceramic or metal bowls are usually best; plastic bowls often turn into chew toys!

Dog Food

Make sure you have some food on hand that the Yorkie is used to eating. If you want to change to another brand, do so gradually over a couple of weeks. Changing right away will give the puppy a belly ache and diarrhea.

Bet You Didn't Know

Take two to three weeks to change foods. The first week, take $3/4$ of the old food to $1/4$ of the new food. By the end of the first week and first part of the second, feed $1/2$ and $1/2$. By the end of the second week to the beginning of the third, feed $1/4$ the old food and $3/4$ the new food. This will get the puppy used to it gradually and ease any gastrointestinal upset.

Collar and Leash

A soft nylon buckle collar will work fine. Many Yorkie owners buy their puppies cat collars, as most dog collars are too big. Cat leashes work well, too. A four-foot leash is a good length.

Identification

Have a collar identification tag with your telephone number on it ready for your puppy when he comes home. You can always get a new one later with the puppy's name on it if you haven't named him by the time you bring him home. Most pet supply stores have machines that engrave the tags while you wait.

Later you can talk to your veterinarian about having a microchip injected under the skin at your Yorkie's shoulder. This is a permanent identification and is recommended by most pet professionals and animal control officers.

Toys!

Your Yorkie will need toys! Active, curious, intelligent Yorkies need stuff to keep them busy, and if there are not toys to play with, everything else becomes a toy! Yorkies like balls, toys that make noise, toys made to be chewed on, and food dispensing toys. When shopping for toys, keep in mind the Yorkie's small size. Choose toys that he can bat around, chase, play with, and chew on.

Bet You Didn't Know

Having too many toys is not better. When a dog has too many toys, he thinks that everything is his! Instead, just give your dog two or three toys at a time and teach him to play with his things. You can rotate toys, however, to keep him interested.

Your Yorkie must, of course, have some toys!

Crate

We'll be talking about how to use a crate in upcoming chapters, so right now just understand that the crate is an awesome training tool for your Yorkie. It will help with housetraining, with preventing many problem behaviors later, and also serves as your Yorkie's bed and special place.

For now, the crate should be big enough for the Yorkie to stand up, turn around, lie down, and get comfortable—and no larger. Cat crates are often big enough. When it comes to crates, bigger is *not* better!

Yorkie Smarts

There are three basic types of crates: plastic, heavy gauge wire, and soft-sided. Get your Yorkie the plastic type; the breed just does better in these. Wire crates are too open and although the soft-sided crates are fine for transporting the dog to the vet or groomer's offices; they don't stand up to daily use like the plastic ones do.

Grooming Supplies

Talk to the groomer you like prior to going shopping for grooming supplies. Not only can she help you choose the right tools, but she may also recommend some specific brands available in your area. She may also be able to get you some tools at a discounted price. It doesn't hurt to ask!

Your long-coated Yorkie will need, at the minimum, the following supplies:

- 🏠 Shampoo and conditioner for long coated puppies
- 🏠 A metal comb for working through long coats
- 🏠 A dematter for getting rid of tangles
- 🏠 Toenail clippers

Don't go overboard and buy out the grooming shop; just get the basics and add to these as you need them or as your groomer recommends them.

Cleaning Supplies

You'll want to have some white vinegar on hand for cleaning up the inevitable housetraining accidents. Paper towels, a scrub brush, and trash bags are necessary, too. Save your plastic grocery bags for picking up after your dog while out for a walk.

Baby Gates or Playpens

Baby gates and playpens were designed to keep human babies and toddlers safe, and they work just as well for puppies. Baby gates can close off rooms and block off hallways so that your puppy can't sneak off somewhere to have a housetraining accident or chew on your shoes. Playpens, although they don't work well for larger puppies that can chew through the sides or hop out, work very well for toy breed dogs. My mother used them quite successfully for several Papillon puppies.

Yorkie Smarts

Garage sales are a great place to pick up playpens or baby gates.

A baby gate is always a good investment.

What Else Do You Need?

Don't buy an expensive dog bed right now, wait until the puppy is grown up and well housetrained. Right now just use a couple of washable old towels.

You might want a pooper scooper for picking up feces in the backyard. Other than that, you're set. Let's bring home that puppy!

The Least You Need to Know

- When making your house safe for your Yorkie, don't forget to look at it from a tiny dog's perspective.
- Make sure your yard and fence are safe, or build a small dog run.
- Find a veterinarian, groomer, and trainer who can help you.
- Make sure you have the supplies on hand you'll need.

Chapter 6

Begin Establishing Household Rules

In This Chapter

- Becoming your Yorkie's leader
- The importance of rules
- Deciding on household rules
- Using rules to prevent problems

You probably wanted a dog as a companion, a friend, and a confidant. Your Yorkie can be all of those things for you, but only after you have cemented your relationship. He is not your equal; he is your dog and needs your leadership. You must teach him that.

You must also teach him how you want him to behave and should begin teaching him as soon as you bring him home. Don't give him a chance to "settle in." That just allows him to misbehave; instead, teach him how you want him to behave right from the beginning.

Deciding on what rules you want to establish in the house will take some thought. Talk to your family and figure out what's important to all of you. Then, everyone must consistently enforce those rules. It's not hard, though, so let's get started.

Your Yorkie Needs a Leader

Your Yorkie's mother was his first teacher. If he bit her too roughly, she would growl at him until he stopped. If he was too rough with his littermates, she would correct him. When he was good, she would lick him with affection. She showed him what it was like to be a dog. She was also his first leader.

Like all youngsters, your Yorkie puppy needs leadership. The *leader* teaches him what the rules are and how to behave. Without leadership, he would have to make up his own rules and would be insecure and fearful or bossy and aggressive; depending upon his personality.

Dog Talk

The **leader** is fair, firm, and demands respect.

Yorkie Smarts

One of the most common mistakes Yorkie owners make is that they spoil their Yorkie instead of lead him. Your Yorkie is tiny, but he's still a dog, and dogs need leaders.

Dogs without good leadership often develop behavior problems. These often are:

- A "bossy" attitude toward the owner, which may include growling, snarling, and snapping.

- Refusal to follow the owner's directions and requests.

- Poor housetraining skills including leg lifting from the males.

- Mounting (humping) behavior from males and females.

Some dog owners want to be their dog's buddy and best friend. That's usually possible; after all, that's why we have dogs! However, this happens later; after the dog is physically grown up and mentally mature and after you have established yourself as your dog's leader. During puppyhood you must be your dog's leader, not his equal or best buddy. He must learn to respect you as well as love you.

How to Be a Leader

I've listed a few things you can do to help your Yorkie understand your leadership. They are not necessarily the things his mother would do; after all, we aren't dogs. But they are things you can do that will help your puppy understand your respective places in the family pack.

🏠 Always eat first; then feed your puppy. In a wild pack—which we know isn't the same as our family but serves as a good example—the leaders of the pack always eat first and best. Then the subordinate pack members eat. To your dog, you should be the giver of the food. This makes you very important. To maximize this importance, you should eat breakfast or dinner first, then give your puppy his meal.

Watch Out!

Don't allow your Yorkie to beg for food; this is a very bad habit that can easily escalate into snapping or food stealing.

🏠 Teach your Yorkie to wait while you walk through doorways first; then give permission for your puppy to either stay behind or to follow you. The puppy who dashes through doorways is going to get into trouble. One day he may dash out the front door ahead of you and end up in the street in front of a car. If he dashes through the door you might step on him and seriously hurt him, or he may trip you, causing you to fall. You have the right to tell him to wait for your permission.

🏠 At least once each day, pick up your Yorkie, roll him over on your lap, and give him a tummy rub. This is a submissive position and even though he probably loves the tummy rub, it's still showing him to be submissive to you. This is good! As the leader, you have to be more dominant than he is.

🏠 Give him permission to do things. If he's picking up his ball, tell him to get his ball and then praise him for doing it. This is what some trainers call "free" training. The puppy was going to do it anyway, so take advantage of it!

Your Yorkie Needs Rules

Household rules give your Yorkie some guidelines as to what is and isn't socially acceptable behavior. One of the most important is housetraining. Your Yorkie should never relieve himself inside your house; that's disgusting, dirty, rude, and disrespectful to you. Another rule is biting. Your Yorkie should never use his teeth on you or anyone else. Again, it is very disrespectful, and even though he's tiny, it's still dangerous.

When you establish these rules very early—as soon as your Yorkie joins your family—he never learns the wrong behavior. For example, do you want him underfoot in the kitchen? Tiny dogs are hard to see when you've got your hands full. Don't allow him in the kitchen now and then try to change the rules in two years. That's not fair! Instead, start teaching the puppy now, as a young puppy, exactly what you expect of him. He's capable of learning; you just need to teach him.

Yorkie Smarts

By 8 to 10 weeks of age, your Yorkie's brain is fully functional and capable of incredible learning. Although he is a baby physically, he is ready and willing to learn.

Is your Yorkie going to be allowed in the kitchen?

Be Consistent

When you establish the household rules, make sure everyone in the household will accept them and enforce them. If your daughter sneaks the Yorkie food from her plate, the dog will continue to beg from the table. If you correct him but your daughter feeds him, he will be confused and his behavior erratic. Everyone must be consistent with the rules.

Posting a list of the rules in a prominent location works for many puppy owners. List a command, such as "No Begging!" so that everyone is using the same language, and a list of the rules themselves. Put it up on the refrigerator where everyone will see it on a daily basis.

Decide on the Rules

When trying to decide what rules you would like to establish, keep in mind what your dog will grow up to be. A toy breed dog is much easier to deal with on the furniture than a giant breed dog with a heavy coat, so you may decide to allow your Yorkie on the furniture. I like to cuddle with my dogs, so they are invited on the furniture. My mother, on the other hand, likes to keep her furniture free of dog hair, so her dogs are not allowed on her furniture.

Your rules should take into account your personal likes and dislikes, your daily routine, and any other desires. Perhaps a half chewed dog bone hidden under a sofa cushion would make you very unhappy; if so, then keep the dog off the furniture.

Listed below are a few suggestions for some household rules that are relatively easy to teach:

🏠 Housetraining is an obvious household rule. All dogs should be well housetrained, but you might be amazed at the number of dogs—especially toy breed dogs—who are not well house-trained. We'll talk about this in great detail in the next chapter, but this should be your first rule.

🏠 No dog, no matter what the size, should use his teeth on people. Biting of any kind—in play or in anger—is to be stopped. This is a dangerous habit so make sure all family members understand.

🏠 We mentioned the dangers of having a tiny Yorkie in the kitchen, but let's look at this again. Although Yorkies can be very quick about staying out from underfoot, they are also easy to step on. If you have a hot pan on the stove or a platter with dinner on it, you don't want to trip over a tiny dog, risking harm to the dog and yourself. Never mind the potential of ruining dinner!

Is your Yorkie to be allowed to beg for food while you're eating? This isn't an acceptable habit, either. The puppy who begs for food usually ends up being a big pest, pawing legs, licking hands, or even stealing food. If you don't want to allow begging, make sure no one feeds the puppy as they eat.

We have also already mentioned the idea of allowing your Yorkie up on the furniture. This is a purely personal decision. Once you make up your mind, however, you can't change a few months down the road or if you get a new sofa.

Many dog owners like to have their dog sleep with them. Unfortunately, this is a bad habit and an especially bad one for Yorkies. Your Yorkie needs his own bed (his crate) and it can be (and should be) in your bedroom. But he should not sleep in your bed, for two reasons. First of all, it is too dangerous for him. A tiny dog can easily get trapped and squashed should an adult roll over on him in the middle of the night. In addition, if the Yorkie sleeps with you, he will think he's your equal—after all, he sleeps in the leader's bed!

Watch Out!

If your Yorkie is already sleeping on the bed and growls at you when you move or ask him to get off the bed, call a dog trainer or behaviorist for help right away. This can be a serious behavior problem that has been known to end up with the dog biting the owner.

Do you want to restrict certain parts of the house? If you wish to keep the puppy out of the kids' rooms so that he won't get into their stuff, that's fine. If you have a nice formal living room, teach him to stay in the family room and restrict him from the living room. In fact, as I've mentioned before, the puppy *does not* and *should not* have free run of the house. To restrict his access, close doors and use baby gates to keep him in the rooms where he is allowed.

What else is important to you? Think about it. What will make life with a dog easier?

Rules Prevent Problems

You want to begin teaching your new Yorkie puppy (or recently adopted dog) the household rules as soon as he joins your household because it is much easier to prevent problems from happening than it is to break bad habits later. If you have ever dieted or tried to stop smoking, you know bad habits can be tough to break, and it's the same with dogs.

Don't let your puppy discover trash cans!

Limit Freedom

If your Yorkie never learns to sneak off down the hall to have a housetraining "accident" it will be much easier to housetrain him—and then ultimately trust him—than it would be if he was allowed to relieve himself in the house. Part of preventing bad behavior is restricting your puppy's access. Keep him in the room with you and keep an eye on him. Don't allow him to sneak off down the hallway where he can get into trouble without you knowing about it.

Keep in mind, with dogs—especially puppies—freedom is not a right. Instead, freedom comes with mental maturity and good behavior. When your Yorkie is well trained and about two years old, then and only then should he have unrestricted access to your house.

Teach Your Yorkie

You also need to teach your puppy what is acceptable and what is not. When he grabs the sofa cushion, take it away from him and hand him one of his toys instead. When he picks up your good leather shoes, take them away, put them in the closet, close the closet door, and hand the puppy one of his toys.

Preventing problems from happening may take some work on your part. You'll have to look at your house and yard from your puppy's perspective: What is attractive to your puppy? Can he reach your potted plants? The hose is fun to chew on did you put it out of his reach? Don't assume that because your Yorkie is small, he can't reach something. Yorkies are very athletic, good climbers, and very smart!

Yorkie Smarts

When your Yorkie is doing something right, give him permission to do it and praise him. For example, if he picks up his toy instead of your shoe, tell him, "Get your toy! Good boy!" Reinforce that good behavior!

The Least You Need to Know

- You must be your Yorkie's leader; a fair but firm leader.
- Household rules teach your Yorkie what is socially acceptable in your home.
- Establish rules that will work for your family and household, and then make sure everyone enforces them consistently.
- Rules can also help prevent problem behavior later.

Chapter 7

Housetraining Can Be a Challenge!

In This Chapter

- 🏠 Housetraining tiny dogs
- 🏠 Putting the crate to good use
- 🏠 Reinforcing good habits
- 🏠 No excuses!

One of the most important social manners your Yorkie needs to learn involves teaching him where he should (and should not) relieve himself. A dog who knows where to relieve himself, where not to relieve himself, and how to try to relieve himself on command is a welcome companion.

As a dog trainer, my students frequently ask me housetraining questions. How can I teach my puppy to go outside? What should I do when my dog has an accident in the house? Why does he have to go outside so often? To many dog owners, housetraining seems to be mystical and incredibly difficult. But it doesn't have to be that way. When I housetrain a new puppy of my own, I go outside with

Dog Talk

Housetraining refers to the process of teaching the dog where to relieve himself and where not to relieve himself.

the puppy so I can teach her, I make up a schedule for trips outside, I restrict the puppy's freedom, and I use a kennel crate. With these tools, my dogs learn *housetraining* rules with little difficulty, and yours should, too.

I am often amazed at the number of Yorkies who are not well housetrained. I have even heard breeders say that it is very difficult or even impossible to housetrain Yorkies (or other toy breed dogs). It may very well be impossible if the breeder or owner doesn't take the time to train the dog correctly. It may also be impossible if the breeder or owner makes too many excuses. However, there is absolutely no reason to live with a dog who isn't housetrained!

Tiny Dogs Can Be Housetrained!

I don't know where the myth got started that toy breed dogs are difficult or impossible to housetrain, but I have heard it said about several breeds, including Yorkies and Papillons. Perhaps because toy breed dogs are so small, an accident is easy to overlook. Or perhaps it's because a toy breed dog has to take more steps than bigger dogs to get to the door. I don't know where the myth came from but I wish it would disappear!

Toy dogs are just as capable of being well housetrained as any other breed of dog of any size. They do sometimes take a little while longer to develop bladder control (they are tiny and that bladder doesn't hold much!) but they are capable of doing it.

Dog Litter Boxes

Litter boxes for tiny dogs have been in use for many years. Most dog owners used large cat litter boxes, complete with either cat litter or dirt. However, in the past few years, commercial dog litter boxes have become available (a little bigger and deeper than cat boxes) complete with litter made specifically for dogs.

I am not a big fan of dog litter boxes except in a few specific situations. In some cases, teaching the dog to use a box in the house seems to teach him to relieve himself in the house rather than "in the house in the box." Too many dogs seem to relieve themselves indiscriminately in the house as well as in the box. If the dog is to be taught to use a box, he must be taught to use it just as rigorously as he would be taught to go outside.

I think litter boxes can work if:

🏠 The owner works long hours and the dog must remain in the house all day with no one to take him outside.

🏠 The owner is an invalid or is housebound.

🏠 The dog and owner live in a climate where the weather would be dangerous for a tiny dog.

If the dog and owner are able to get outside on a regular basis, I prefer teaching the dog to relieve himself outside. It's easier, usually more dependable, and more natural to the dog.

A Crate Can Help

A crate (often called a kennel or a kennel crate) is a travel carrier for dogs. Originally used for dogs being transported on airplanes, they are now used to help dogs learn housetraining skills. A crate works by taking advantage of the puppy's own instincts to keep his bed clean. Very few puppies or dogs will soil their bed, so they learn (with your help) to not go in their bed and to go where you wish them to go.

Watch Out!
Puppies bought from a pet store often have trouble learning crate training because they spend too much time in a cage. Because they must relieve themselves in the cage, they lose their inhibition about soiling their bed.

Three Types of Crates

There are three types of crates available and each has its own good points and bad points. You need to look at your needs and the needs of your dog and choose which crate would work best.

The first type of crate (and the most popular) is made of plastic or fiberglass. It has a metal barred door and barred windows for ventilation on each side. These come in two parts, top and bottom, and are easily cleaned. They are relatively lightweight and although somewhat bulky, are easily stored. Because they have solid sides, these crates provide the puppy with a feeling of security; much like a den.

Heavy gauge wire crates are more like a cage. The open sides provide good air circulation and in hot weather, this is wonderful. Because they are open, though, some dogs—especially many tiny Yorkies—feel exposed and vulnerable. These crates are heavy, although most brands do fold up flat. They usually have a metal tray in the bottom that can be pulled out to be cleaned.

The third type is often called a carry bag rather than a crate, but it's essentially a soft-sided crate for carrying toy breed dogs, cats, ferrets, and other small pets. These can be very useful for transporting your Yorkie to the vet's office or groomer, but these should not be used for daily training. With the soft sides, these collapse too easily, can be chewed through, and don't provide enough security for you or your puppy. Keep in mind that if you want to use these for traveling, the soft-sided carriers provide no protection to your Yorkie if you are in an accident.

Yorkie Smarts
You may wish to have a plastic crate for use at home and a soft-sided carrying bag for errands around town.

Crate Size

Choose a crate that will allow your puppy to stand up, turn around, and stretch out. Too much room is not better. If the crate is too big, the puppy can relieve himself in a back corner and still have room to get away from it. The purpose of using a crate to housetrain your puppy is to utilize his instinct to keep his bed clean. A cat crate will probably fit your tiny Yorkie just fine!

Your Yorkie's Place

As your Yorkie is introduced to the crate, it will become his own personal space. It's his den or cave—a place where he can hide his favorite toys or bones. He can retreat to his crate when he's tired or doesn't feel good. He will sleep in his crate at night and will spend some time there during the day when you're unable to supervise him.

Keep It Positive!

The crate should never be used for punishment, however. Never put your Yorkie in his crate as you are scolding him. Never yell at him or berate him while he's in the crate; not only will these episodes make him think the crate is a bad place, but those types of corrections are not good dog training techniques.

Introducing the Crate

You are going to want your Yorkie to think the crate is a fun place all of his own, so how you introduce him to it is important. Place the crate in the living room and fasten the door open so it can't close unexpectedly and startle him.

Have a few dog treats, and toss them one at a time toward the crate. Let him grab and eat those treats. A little while later, toss a treat or two into the crate and let him get those. Later still or even the next day, let him chase a couple of treats into the crate.

When he will go in and out with no trouble, start feeding him in the crate, but continue to keep the door open. When he will eat in the crate with no fuss, close the door behind him. Do *not* let him out if he throws a fit! Open the door only when he is calm and quiet. If he cries, barks, and scratches at the door, ignore him.

Using the Crate

Put the crate in your bedroom at night so your Yorkie can hear you, smell you, and be close to you all night. This is eight hours of closeness that you probably couldn't find the time for at any other time of day. Yorkies need time with their owner, and although these night time hours don't require you to do anything except sleep, to your dog, they are wonderful.

In addition, with the puppy close to you, you can hear him if he gets restless and needs to go outside. If he doesn't have to go outside and is just moving around, you can reach over, tap the top of the crate and tell him, "No! Quiet!" However, if your puppy's restlessness continues, take him outside.

During the day, put the puppy in his crate for a few minutes here and there; whenever you are too busy to supervise him. Since he has to spend many hours in his crate at night, try to limit his time in it during the day to short time periods. Twenty minutes here and thirty minutes there are okay as long as he gets plenty of attention, exercise, and time with you in between times in the crate.

Don't Abuse It!

Other than at night, don't leave your Yorkie in the crate for more than two to three hours at a time. During the day, he needs time to stretch his legs, run, and play.

If you and other family members work all day, make some arrangements for your dog. Perhaps he can go to a doggy day care or you can ask a neighbor to take him out and walk him. Many teenage kids will walk dogs for a few dollars a week. If you can't make other arrangements, then a secure, safe, covered dog run might be the best answer.

Preventing Problems

A crate can help you prevent problems from happening. If you can prevent the puppy from learning bad habits, training will be much easier. In addition, your puppy won't be able to cause as much damage, which reduces your—and your puppy's—stress!

When you can't supervise your Yorkie puppy, put him outside in a safe place in the yard or put him in his crate. By ensuring he doesn't get into trouble, you're preventing problem behavior. He will never learn that it's fun to chew up the sofa cushions if he never gets a chance to do it! By preventing the bad behavior, you can also ensure the dog learns good habits. The puppy learns to chew on the toys you give him rather than learning to be destructive.

Housetraining Your Yorkie

With all the conflicting advice and misinformation about housetraining that bombards new puppy owners, it's amazing that so many dogs do eventually become well housetrained. However, housetraining doesn't have to be mysterious or confusing. If you understand your puppy's need to keep his bed clean, limit your puppy's freedom, teach him what you want, where you want it, and set a good schedule; your puppy will cooperate.

Take Him Outside

Take your Yorkie outside where you want him to relieve himself. Stand outside with him, but don't interact with him. When the puppy starts to sniff and circle, just watch. After he has started to relieve himself, tell him softly, "Go potty! Good boy to go potty!"

(Using, of course, whatever vocabulary you wish to use.) When he has completed his business, praise him even more.

You'll need to go out with him to this particular spot every time he needs to go for several weeks. Yes, weeks! You cannot simply send the puppy outside. If you do, how do you know he has done what he needs to do? How can you teach him the command if you aren't there? And how can you praise him for doing what needs to be done if, again, you aren't there? Even worse, if you let him back inside when he hasn't relieved himself, it's then your fault if he comes in and has an accident.

Many dog owners come to my training classes complaining about their dog's lack of housetraining skills and, invariably, they say, "I send my dog outside but when he comes back in, he goes on the floor!" In these situations, the dog is going outside alone. The owner lets the dog in a few minutes later but has no idea whether the dog has actually relieved himself outside. (Even if he has, the owner wasn't there to praise the dog for going in the right place or to teach him the proper command.) When the dog is allowed back in the house and relieves himself on the floor, he is yelled at. Granted getting yelled at is negative attention, but it's still attention. In these cases, I tell the owners they have housetrained their dog all right; they have trained him to go in the house!

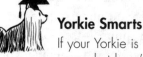

Yorkie Smarts

If your Yorkie is young but hasn't had an accident in a while, don't assume he's housetrained. Instead, simply realize you are doing everything correctly!

Housetraining is a very important skill, and many dogs (including many Yorkies) end up at animal control shelters all over the country because they haven't been well housetrained. Take your time while your Yorkie is young and teach this correctly; it's too important to take lightly.

Using the "Go Potty!" Command

It's important that your Yorkie puppy understand his command to relieve himself. If you take the puppy (or later, the dog) to visit someone, it's very nice to be able to tell the dog to relieve himself before going inside the house. The same thing works when you're traveling. If you stop to get gas, you can then tell the dog to try and relieve himself, and even if his bladder isn't full, he can try.

Start using a command when you first start housetraining the puppy. Tell him "Go potty!" (Using the vocabulary that is comfortable to you) and praising him when he does relieve himself. "Good boy to go potty!"

As his housetraining gets better and more reliable, use the commands when you're out on walks so he learns to go potty in different places. Some puppies learn that they are to relieve themselves only in their backyard, and their owners have a difficult time teaching them that it's okay to do it elsewhere. So teach the puppy that when you give him this command, he is to try, even if he can only squeeze out a drop!

Dogs Are Creatures of Habit

Dogs, like many people, are creatures of habit. Housetraining is much easier if the puppy eats, sleeps, and goes outside on a fairly regular schedule. Variations are allowed of course, but not too many.

Keep in mind that a very young puppy will need to eat two to three times per day. He'll need to go outside to relieve himself after each meal. He'll also need to go outside after playing, when waking up from a nap, and about every two hours in between. After a nap or after sleeping in the night, carry your puppy outside, as he may need to relieve himself right away.

Take all of these things into account when you set up a schedule. Take into consideration, too, your normal routine. You may have to

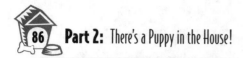
make some adjustments in your routine to get the puppy outside often enough, but that goes hand in hand with having a puppy!

As your Yorkie puppy gets older and develops more bladder and bowel control, he'll be able to go longer between trips outside, but this is a gradual process. Many puppies can be considered house-trained and reliable by five to six months of age as long as they aren't required to hold it too long. However, it is not unusual for some puppies to need a strict schedule and many trips outside until six, seven, and even eight months of age. Just as some children potty train at different ages and rates; so do puppies. A puppy is house-trained and reliable when he is ready and able to do it.

When Your Yorkie's Gotta Go!

Once you've set up a schedule for your Yorkie puppy, you need to follow it. In addition, you want to teach him to notify you when he needs to go out.

When I have a puppy at home, I use my voice a lot as a training tool. As I walk the puppy toward the back door, I will ask him, "Rover, do you have to go potty?" in a high-pitched, happy tone of voice. As the puppy reacts to my tone of voice and as he learns the words, he will get excited and dash toward the door. I will praise him for that. I will praise him again when he relieves himself in the proper place outside.

Watch Out!

I don't teach my dogs to bark when they want to go outside because, as a dog trainer, I hear many complaints about barking dogs. Teaching a dog to bark to go outside can be emphasizing a potential behavior problem.

As the dog gains more control and can go longer between trips outside, I will check with him once in a while, "Do you have to go potty?" If he does, he will dance and wiggle and head toward the door. I will, of course, praise him and let him out. If he just stares at me, that means he doesn't need to go right now, thank you!

Later, as they get older, my dogs will come and stare at me when they want my attention. When I turn to look at them, they will tell me they need something. Kes will stare, turn toward the door and look back at me as if to say, "Follow me, Mom!" Dax will bring me a toy. I will then ask the dog, "Do you need to go potty?" If the answer is yes, then I'll let him outside.

Take your time with training, however. It takes time and maturity for the dog to learn to ask you for help. Some Yorkies don't want to leave the people in the house long enough to go outside, and so they try and hold their bladder too long. You have to be aware of the dog's schedule and make sure he gets outside in time.

No Excuses!

Many Yorkie owners seem to be masters at making excuses. I don't know if it's because their dogs are so tiny, or so cute, but excuses are always readily available. "He had an accident because he ate too much!" or "It is too cold/hot/windy/rainy/snowy outside." Excuses, however, won't housetrain your dog.

Now, I understand that accidents happen. Perhaps you won't be watching the puppy closely enough and he will urinate on the floor. When an accident does happen, you must handle it very carefully. It's important the puppy learns that urinating and defecating are not wrong, but the place where he did it was wrong. If the puppy feels that relieving himself is wrong, then he will become sneaky about it, and you will find puddles in strange places, including behind the furniture.

If you come upon the puppy as he is having an accident, then use a verbal correction, "Acck! What are you doing?" Scoop him up and take him outside. Then clean up the mess, but do not let him watch you clean it up. If you find an accident after the fact, don't correct the puppy—it's too late.

Excuses won't housetrain your dog.

Don't rub the puppy's nose in his mess—that teaches him that the urine or defecation is the problem, and that's not what you want him to learn. Don't drag him to his mess and shake him or yell at him; that will only confuse him. Remember, the act of relieving himself is not wrong; it's the act of relieving himself *in the house* that's wrong. Make sure your message is very clear.

If your puppy is having a few accidents in the house, you need to make sure you are going outside with him so that you can praise him when he relieves himself outside. Make sure he knows when and where it is right. You will also need to pay more attention to the puppy's schedule; are you getting him outside enough and at the right times? You may also be giving him too much freedom. Make sure he stays in the room with you and cannot sneak off to another room.

Successful housetraining is based on setting the puppy up for success by allowing few accidents to happen, and then praising the puppy when he relieves himself outside.

Should You Install a Doggy Door?

Doggy doors can be very effective for adult dogs who are left home alone for many hours each day. The dog can go outside to relieve himself or to lie in the sun and can get back inside when he so desires.

I don't recommend doggy doors for puppies, however, because the door will eliminate you from the training process, and you are a vital part of it. You need to go outside with your puppy to teach him the command to relieve himself. You also need to praise him when he does relieve himself in the correct place.

Dog Talk

A **doggy door** is a small door (or flap) that can be installed so that your Yorkie can go in and out as he pleases without any assistance from you. It should open to a safe, secure area.

In addition, if he goes in and out on his own, do you know whether or not he has relieved himself? If you're getting ready to take him for a car ride, do you know whether he has a full bladder or not?

Watch Out!

If you live in an area with hawks or eagles, don't use a doggy door unless it opens out into a covered, secure dog run. Never let your Yorkie go out to an open backyard without you.

A doggy door gives a puppy entirely too much freedom. He ends up with free access to the house and, to a puppy, that's an awful lot of fun!

Be Patient

All puppies need time to grow and develop bladder and bowel control, so be patient with your puppy's housetraining. Just establish a schedule that seems to work for you and your puppy and stick to it. If you follow the right schedule, your puppy will do fine. However, the lack of accidents doesn't mean you can ease up on your supervision; instead, a lack of accidents means your schedule is good! If you ease up too soon, your puppy will have some accidents, and you'll have to start all over again.

A schedule that works for you and your puppy, along with careful supervision and lots of patience, will work. Puppies do eventually grow up, and all your efforts will pay off when you find that you have a well-housetrained, reliable dog.

The Least You Need to Know

- A crate will help your Yorkie develop bowel and bladder control.
- Teach your dog to relieve himself outside and on command.
- Establish a schedule for eating, sleeping, playing, and for going outside.
- Be patient. Housetraining takes time.

Chapter 8

Socialization Is Vital

In This Chapter

🏠 Taking the time to socialize

🏠 When and how to socialize

🏠 Understanding fear periods

🏠 Making socialization a life-long adventure

Yorkshire Terriers should be, according to the breed standard, alert and self-confident. Yorkies are often called the "King of Terriers" because even though they are tiny, they have an awesome attitude. A Yorkie's attitude should shout, "Hey, look at me!" Unfortunately, the tendency of many Yorkie owners is to coddle and protect their dogs—especially puppies—and this creates problem behaviors.

A Yorkie who is protected from the world learns to fear the world. Everything becomes frightening. The Yorkie will be timid and fearful, shying away from noises, sights, people, and other dogs. A fearful dog also has the potential of becoming a fear biter. A fearful dog is not a happy dog.

Yorkies need to be well *socialized* to develop their confident, "look at me" attitude. A well-socialized dog will be aware of the world, know his place in it, and know how to cope. A dog who has been coddled and overprotected will become fearful, timid, and shy. A dog who has been overly protected watches the world go by while a well-socialized dog participates in it.

The Importance of Socialization

Last year I had two Yorkies enroll in a puppy kindergarten class at the same time. Both had gone to their new homes between 10 and 12 weeks of age and both were 14 weeks old when enrolling in class. The similarities stopped there, however.

The first puppy, I'll call him Rover (to protect the owner's identity) had been coddled in his first few weeks at home. He was never allowed to walk outside unless it was to relieve himself. Rover's owner had never let him meet other dogs, even well known, healthy, vaccinated dogs. He went to the veterinarian's office, his owner's office, and that was it. When he came to class, Rover was worried about everything, and when I told her to set him on the ground, he tried to climb up her leg to get back into her arms. As soon as I turned away from her, she picked him back up again.

Dog Talk

Socialization is the process of introducing a puppy to the world around him, and continuing the process with an adult dog.

The other puppy, Fido (again, name changed to protect the owner), was taken everywhere by his owner. He had already been for walks at the local harbor where he saw boats, heard boat motors, saw sea gulls and pelicans fly overhead, and where many people petted him. He had met the neighbor's dogs and played with a couple of the neighbor's grandchildren. When Fido came to class, he trotted in on the leash, visited with the other puppies, and wanted the puppies' owners to pet him.

Both of these puppies had been born with the terrier "devil may care" attitude, and I know this because I called the breeders. Because Fido's owner treated him like a dog (rather than a precious jewel) and introduced him to the world around him, he has graduated from puppy and basic obedience class, finished therapy dog training, and is now a certified therapy dog, visiting people in nursing homes and hospitals. He is well adjusted, happy, and has the "look at me" attitude.

Rover, on the other hand, dropped out of puppy class. He is still very fearful and rarely goes anywhere unless he's in his owner's arms. The groomer says she has a difficult time with him because he's afraid of the clippers, her scissors, and the other grooming tools. He has snapped at her on several occasions. His owner makes many excuses for him but has yet to admit that she caused her dog's behavior problems by not socializing him and by overprotecting him.

Why Is Socialization Important?

When a puppy is introduced to the world around him, he develops skills that enable him to cope with that world. When a motorcycle zooms past, a well-socialized dog may look, cock his ears, and then process that information, "Ah ha. I've seen those before," and will continue walking. A dog who has not been well socialized may react with panic, pulling on the leash while trying to run away, or worse yet, he may try to slip out of the leash. He may bark and growl at the motorcycle, or react negatively to those around him since he can't get to the motorcycle.

Socialization to the sights, sounds, and smells of the world around him enable the dog to become familiar with the world. He learns to think (instead of react) when things happen. He develops confidence in himself and trusts that you are there to help him.

Let gentle people pet your Yorkie.

How and When to Socialize

Much of your Yorkie's socialization can be as simple as allowing him to meet new people. Take him outside and introduce him to your neighbors. Let him meet the neighborhood kids, the retirees down the street, and the teenagers across the way. Let him meet people of all ages, sizes, shapes, and ethnic backgrounds.

You can also plan outings so that he can go different places and meet other people:

🏠 Go for walks to different places. Walk in a park, along the river, by the beach, and in the hills. Walk in housing tracts and in rural areas when possible.

- Many businesses are great opportunities for socialization. An ice cream store, pizza place, or even a tire store all have people coming in and out—most of whom will want to meet your puppy!

- Take him to family get-togethers. Let Grandma, Grandpa, the aunts, uncles, and all the kids pet him and play with him.

- Take him to the pet supply store with you. Let him meet the sales clerks as well as other customers, and then reward him by letting him pick out a new toy. In the pet store, he can also learn how to walk on slippery floors and see things he wouldn't see at home (like display shelves and stacks of aquariums). He can also learn to walk next to a shopping cart—something that is very different!

- Take him to the veterinarian's office even when he doesn't have an appointment. Just walk him in, have the receptionist give him a treat, and then leave again. That makes the vet's office something special instead of something scary!

Watch Out!

Don't introduce your puppy to every dog in town; be selective. Socialize only with healthy, well-vaccinated, well-behaved dogs who are safe with puppies.

See, Smell, and Hear

Introduce your Yorkie puppy to as much as you can; not all at once, of course, but throughout puppyhood. Let him become familiar, comfortable, and confident about the world around him.

Yorkie Smarts

Your Yorkie's adult personality is shaped by several things: his breed and genetic heritage, his mother's care, the socialization and training he receives, and you.

While protecting him from harm (without reinforcing fear) let him see, hear, or smell the following things:

In the house:

The vacuum cleaner

The dishwasher, garbage disposal, and trash compactor

The washing machine and dryer

The hair dryer

A plastic garbage bag being shook open

A crumpled paper bag

A broom and mop being used

A plastic bag being popped

A metal cookie sheet being dropped to the floor

Children's toys, including some that make noise

Balls of various sizes, shapes, and colors

Outside:

A car engine being revved

The trash truck out front

A motorcycle zooming down the street

People (and kids) on bicycles, skateboards, and inline skates

In the backyard:

The lawn mower

A weed whacker and leaf blower

A rake being used

The hose being shook out, untangled, and curled up again

Water coming from the hose (but not squirted at the puppy!)

Metal and plastic trash cans, including the lids

🏠 Other pets or animals:

Big dogs and little dogs; hairy dogs and short-haired dogs

Cats

Rabbits

Ferrets

Turtles and tortoises

Horses, goats, cows, or sheep

🏠 In addition, you can help your Yorkie by helping him do the following:

Walk him up and down some stairs

Walk him over a wooden footbridge

Walk him over a metal manhole cover

Take him on an elevator

Walk him on carpet, artificial turf, slippery floors, and rubber matting.

Keep It Happy!

The key to socialization is to introduce your Yorkie to the world around him without frightening him. That means your tone of voice should be happy and upbeat; sound like someone just offered you your favorite ice cream cone, "Ice cream!"

If your puppy reacts fearfully to something, do not "save" him. If you hug him or coddle him, or say "It's okay, sweetheart, don't worry," he'll take all that reassurance and assume you're praising him for his fear. In other words, you were telling him in human terms not to be afraid, but he was understanding in canine terms that he was right to be afraid. A common misunderstanding.

To make sure there's no misunderstanding, be very upbeat. When something startles him, say in an "ice cream" tone of voice, "Wow! What was that?" and when you can, walk him up to it.

"Here, look at this." Touch the motorcycle, or flapping sheet on the clothesline, or the child on the skateboard. Encourage him to come close and sniff the scary thing or person, and when he's brave, praise him!

What *Not* to Do

Don't try to introduce your puppy to everything all at once. Overwhelming him is just as bad as not socializing him. This should be a gradual process, taking place over the first few months of his life.

In his first week at home, especially if he comes home during the eighth week of life (during his first fear period) introduce him to things around the house. You can make sure he isn't frightened or, if he is, that you don't reinforce those fears. Keep things upbeat, happy, and matter of fact.

During his second week at home, take him outside a little more, introduce him to a few things around the neighborhood, and let him meet some new people. There are some things you must control, however, to protect your puppy:

- 🏠 Don't let people—kids or adults—run around the puppy. This could be frightening or overstimulating.

- 🏠 Don't let kids scream and yell while playing with the puppy. Again, this is overstimulating or scary.

- 🏠 Don't let people grab your puppy and hug him.
- 🏠 Don't let kids throw themselves on the puppy.
- 🏠 Don't allow people to grab his face, put their face in his, blow in his face, or stare at him.

Remember, the whole idea is to make these outings fun and to build social skills, not scare the puppy.

Watch for Fear Periods

During your Yorkie puppy's eighth week of life, he will go through what is called a *fear period*. At this age, he has become very aware of the world around him, and sometimes that world is very scary. It's important at this age that you try to prevent frightening things from happening, but if they do, don't reinforce that fear. If you do, the puppy will remain afraid and that fear will stay with him.

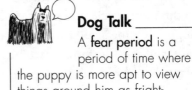

Dog Talk

A **fear period** is a period of time where the puppy is more apt to view things around him as frightening.

Many breeders prefer to keep Yorkie puppies until they are 10 to 12 weeks of age so that this fear period doesn't cause ongoing problems later in life. If the breeder is dedicated to socializing the puppy well, that's no problem. The puppy can still bond with you and your family at 10 to 12 weeks of age. However, if the breeder isn't taking the time to socialize the puppy, you would be better off bringing the puppy home with you, watching for this fear period, and coping with it and the socialization yourself.

Coping with a Fear Period

Yorkie puppies show they are in this fear period in many different ways. Some will become cautious about everything; approaching things (even familiar things) tentatively. Other puppies will be more selective; being bold about some things and cautious with others.

You can do several different things to handle fear. First of all, talk to your Yorkie puppy in either a calm and matter of fact tone of voice, or you can use a higher-pitched, fun tone of voice. Just don't use a soothing tone of voice that he might mistake as sympathy; that will only reinforce his fears.

You can also try to distract your puppy by turning him away from what scared him; and when you turn him away, offer him a toy or a treat, "Here! What's this? Here's your ball!" Distract him and make him think about something else.

If the object of his fear is accessible, you might want to walk up to it, touch it, and show him it isn't as scary as he thought. Walk up to the motorcycle and pat it (as if you were petting it) and tell your puppy, "Come see!" If he walks close to it, praise him enthusiastically and tell him how brave he is! If he is really afraid, however, and plants his feet, don't force him up to the object of his fear. You can touch it, but let him sit back and look at it. When he's ready, then let him go up to it. If you force him, you may just make the fear that much worse.

Yorkie Smarts
Carry some dog treats in your pocket and, when your puppy meets someone new, let them offer him a treat or two.

Bet You Didn't Know
When introducing your puppy to a friendly adult dog, don't hold his leash tight, restraining him. Instead, give him some slack in his leash so that he can move around.

Your Yorkie puppy will go through other fear periods as he grows up. Some puppies have a small fear period at about four months of age and others go through one at about 14 months. You might think that a dog 14 months of age is grown up, but that's not true. A 14-month-old dog is an adolescent—a teenager—and is still mentally immature.

This is usually the last fear period most dogs go through; however, it should still be treated the same way you did when he was a puppy.

Socialization Is a Process

Socialization is an ongoing process that's important for puppies, but it shouldn't stop just because a puppy has grown up. I'm always exposing my dogs—even my adult dogs—to different things. On any given weekend, we may play on the playground, go to a different park, meet a parade horse, or watch a marching band. My dogs have swum in the ocean, sniffed noses with a Budweiser Clydesdale, visited with Alzheimer's patients, and ridden on a San Francisco cable car. My dogs have hiked in the Sierra Nevada Mountains, walked through the forests in the Appalachian Mountains, hiked in meadows, and explored deserts. They have attended the county fair and walked in local Christmas parades. And they take it all in stride.

My grandmother always said that parents should raise their children to take the path they want them to take. Basically it's the same with puppies. Raise your puppy to take that path with you; if you like to do things and go places, introduce your Yorkie puppy to those things now and, when he's grown up, he'll be right there by your side.

When Your Veterinarian Disagrees!

Your veterinarian will probably tell you to keep your Yorkie puppy at home until he has finished all his vaccinations. Until then, he may be at risk of picking up a contagious disease from unvaccinated, unhealthy dogs. In this chapter, however, I have just emphasized the importance of early socialization. Obviously, there is a disagreement here.

Your veterinarian is concerned about your puppy's health, and he or she has a justifiable concern. As a dog trainer, I am concerned about the serious consequences of a lack of socialization.

Unsocialized dogs run the risk of developing severe behavior problems, including fear-based aggression. Granted, not all unsocialized dogs are fear biters; nor are all fear biters unsocialized. However, there is a strong enough relationship to show us that socialization must be begun when the dog is a puppy. The other advantages of socialization are just frosting on the cake.

So how can you protect your puppy's health and socialize him? First of all, don't take him anywhere there are other dogs, especially potentially unvaccinated dogs, until your puppy has had at least two full sets of shots. These vaccines should include distemper, hepatitis, leptospirosis, parvovirus, and para-influenza. Most puppies have, at that point, good immunities. Most kindergarten puppy classes will not allow puppies to attend until they have had these two sets of shots.

Watch Out!

Don't think that only stray dogs are unvaccinated; your neighbors' dogs may not be up to date on their shots. To protect your puppy, be forward and ask!

When you have a puppy, it's important to be proactive in ensuring your dog's safety. Be assertive when necessary, and ask questions of other dog owners *before* you let the dogs sniff each other, "When were your dog's last shots?" If the dog owners get upset, too bad! It's your puppy's health, and you have every right to protect him.

Most of the dangers to your puppy's health come from unvaccinated dogs and their wastes. Keep him away from unknown dogs, and don't let your puppy sniff other dogs' feces and urine. Keep him away and pull him away if he tries to sniff.

You can keep your Yorkie puppy safe by being aware and careful, yet still get him the socialization he needs for good mental health.

The Least You Need to Know

- Take the time to socialize your Yorkie; its importance cannot be emphasized enough.

- Begin socialization early and keep it upbeat and fun.

- Fear periods are normal; just don't give in to them.

- Socialization should continue through puppyhood and into adulthood.

Part 3

The Healthy Yorkshire Terrier

The Yorkie's magnificent coat requires daily grooming and care. We'll take a look at what must be done and how you can do it. Some people decide to keep their Yorkie's coat short, and we'll take a look at the pros and cons of that, too.

Good nutrition is vital to a healthy coat and a healthy body underneath the coat. What is good nutrition? We'll look at what dogs need in their diet and how to choose the right kind of dog food, supplements, and treats.

This section will cover other health concerns as well, including diseases, parasites, vaccinations, and emergency first aid. We'll also discuss some health problems known to plague some Yorkies so that you can identify their symptoms and understand how they are commonly treated.

Grooming Your Yorkie

In This Chapter

- 🏠 Taking care of that Yorkie coat
- 🏠 The grooming process
- 🏠 Trimming toenails
- 🏠 Cleaning ears, teeth, and more

As we saw in the breed standard in Chapter 2, that luscious, flowing coat is a big part of what makes Yorkshire Terriers so unique. The blue and tan coloring, the long coat parted down the back, and the long hair around the face are trademarks of the breed. Sure, there are other breeds with similar coats, but none are quite as special as the Yorkie's.

Unfortunately, this coat requires quite a bit of care. Other health chores, such as nail trimming, ear cleaning, and tooth brushing, should become a part of your daily and weekly routine.

As these become a part of your routine, your Yorkie will learn to accept them instead of fight them. With a regular routine, it's also much easier to keep an eye on your Yorkie's health because as you groom him, you can watch for problems such as ear infections, lumps and bumps, cuts or scratches, or fleas and ticks.

Ah, That Yorkie Coat!

The Yorkshire Terrier's long, flowing coat is a trademark of the breed, but it can also be a problem. That luscious coat requires daily care or it will quickly turn into a matted mess. *Matts* form most quickly where the dog's body moves: on the collar under the neck or behind the ears, the armpits of the front legs, and between the back legs. If the dog has an itch and scratches or chews, matts will form quickly in those spots, too.

Dog Talk

Matts are tangles of hair that become tight and almost solid. Often they cannot be brushed out and instead must be trimmed out of the coat.

Matts seem to have a life of their own. Some dog owners compare them to space aliens! Once a matt has formed, it seems as if its goal is to attract all the nearby hair, and get that hair to join the matt so that the matt can grow as large as possible as quickly as possible!

Once the matt has formed, it becomes an irritant to the dog because it pulls on the skin and rubs against the skin. This causes the dog to bother it, making the matt even more of an irritant, and a vicious cycle begins.

Because matts are so unsightly, cause the dog so much bother, and must often be trimmed out of the coat (leaving a chunk missing from the coat) it's best to prevent matts from forming by brushing the coat daily. Daily brushing can catch tiny tangles before they turn into full-fledged matts.

The Yorkie's long coat can also attract debris. The silky coat makes it less attractive to debris than some other softer, more cottony coats, but it can still pick up twigs, burrs, grass seeds, and other debris during walks and romps in the park. Therefore, after walks and outside play sessions, and certainly at least once a day, check the coat for debris. If left in the coat, debris can cause matts to form.

Maintaining the Look

Many Yorkie owners find the breed's long, flowing coat a little more than they can handle. If you love the look of the coat but find it difficult to keep up with, there is a way to lessen the grooming chores yet keep the appearance of the coat.

Your groomer can help you make the coat easier to care for by keeping the coat on the top and sides of the body long and shaving it underneath. The chest, belly, inside of the legs, and groin area are shaved short. The top coat then falls over the shaved areas, preserving the look of the breed, but with easier care. You'll still have to groom your Yorkie daily, but you'll have far less hair to deal with.

If you think this might be something you would like, talk to your groomer. The two of you can look at your dog and decide how much coat you want taken off. It might take a couple of grooming sessions to get it right, but the coat always grows back, so if you don't like the cut, all you have to do is wait a while!

 Yorkie Smarts

Find a groomer you are comfortable with and then keep the lines of communication open. Talk to her. Tell her what you like and dislike. She can't help you with your dog unless she knows what kind of help you need.

Make It Shorter!

Yorkie puppies, with their shorter, softer coat, are very cute, and some owners of adult Yorkies like to preserve that look by having their Yorkie's coat trimmed. Although the shorter coat doesn't have the rich look of the adult Yorkie's long, flowing coat, the short coat is easier to care for.

Trimming the coat usually consists of trimming the longer hairs to a length decided upon between you and your groomer. Usually the coat is scissored (rather than trimmed with clippers) and may be from two to four inches in length. This gives the suggestion of the Yorkie coat but shortens it to a length that's easier to maintain. The coat is usually trimmed uniformly over the body, although some owners prefer to keep a little more length on the face to maintain that unique Yorkie expression.

I have seen some Yorkies trimmed very short—down to about an inch of coat or even shorter—and although these little dogs look quite athletic and spunky, they just don't look like Yorkies. However, some groomers have said that taking Yorkies down short is not as unusual as we might think. During flea season and hot weather, it's much easier to care for a short-coated dog than one with a full coat. Busy, active people also find the short coat easier to maintain. Although a short coat isn't the trademark of the breed, I would much rather see the dog's coat short and well cared for than see a long coat that has been neglected.

It's up to you. What's most important is that your Yorkie is clean, healthy, and well cared for. So do what is best for you and your Yorkie.

Bet You Didn't Know

If you like a short coat, you can learn to clip your dog yourself. You'll need a good set of clippers made for dog hair (not human hair), a couple of different blades and blade guards for cutting the hair at different lengths, a book or video on grooming (several are available), and lots of patience!

That Gorgeous Showcoat!

Yorkshire Terriers who participate in conformation dog shows have long, flowing coats that drag on the ground. You can't even see legs or paws; just movement under the coat. That coat doesn't just happen; it takes considerable maintenance.

Because the coat can be damaged easily—even by daily activities—conformation show dogs wear their coat up in curlpapers. Curlpapers are those lightweight papers beauticians use to wrap around hair before it is wrapped around curlers. For Yorkies, the hair is not curled, but the curlpapers are used to protect the hair so it isn't damaged. Show dogs wear their coat up in curlpapers whenever they are not in a show.

This takes a lot of work on the part of the dog's owner or handler, and patience on the dog's part. Instead of a flowing coat, the dog lives with a coat tied up in tiny bundles all over his face and body. Obviously, getting a dog ready for conformation shows requires some sacrifices, and this is one of them.

Most dog owners don't need to go through this with their dog; it's not necessary and is entirely too much work. Your dog can still be attractive and a good representative of the breed without that kind of sacrifice.

Yorkie Smarts

If you think you would like to participate in conformation dog shows and would like to learn how to prepare the coat, talk to your dog's breeder. He or she can guide you through the process.

Grooming Is a Process

Grooming your Yorkie is a process, and it's important not to skip any steps. If you do, or if you try to rush it, you could end up with a bigger mess than you started with. So let's take this from the beginning.

Grooming Tools

The first things you will need are some grooming tools. Make sure you have the following items on hand:

🏠 **Shampoo and conditioner.** Use only gentle products made for long-coated dogs (or puppies).

🏠 **Hair dryer.** Make sure there is a cool or low setting.

🏠 **Grooming spray.** This is a spray that helps the comb go through a tangled coat. Your groomer can recommend a product.

🏠 **Comb.** A metal comb with both widely spaced teeth on one side and narrow teeth on the other is great. You can find this at a well-stocked pet supply store.

🏠 **Pin brush.** This brush has metal teeth with rounded ends. The teeth are often set into a rubber inset on the head to cushion the teeth.

🏠 **Dematter.** This brush has three or four curved blades that are sharp on one side. It is used to brush through tangled hair.

🏠 **Nail clippers.** Get a small pair of dog nail clippers. I prefer the ones that look like curved scissors.

If you have any questions about buying any of these items, talk to your groomer. I'll explain how to use these tools as we go along.

Brushing and Combing

Decide first of all where you want to groom your Yorkie. Although it may be easy to do this with your dog on your lap, sometimes it's really better to have a set place. When you do the grooming in the same place each time, your Yorkie learns what to expect and you can teach him how you want him to behave while you groom him.

I prefer to have my dogs stand on a table when I groom them. I can then stand and move around the table, or sit next to the table, all the while easily seeing the dog. I have the dogs stand on a piece of nonskid material sold as cupboard liners. It's inexpensive, can be washed easily, and most importantly, helps the dogs keep their footing on the table.

Once your dog is on the table, teach him to stand quietly by holding him, talking to him gently, and keeping him in position. If he lays down, tries to jump off the table, or squirms, use your voice to correct him, "Acck! No!" and then reposition him while talking gently to him, "That's a good boy."

When your dog will stand on the table, examine him. If there are tangles in his coat, get those out first. Work them with your fingers to see if you can pull them apart, then try the dematter. A little squirt of grooming spray sometimes helps. If you can't get the matt untangled, you may need to trim it out. Put your fingers between the matt and your dog's skin so that you don't cut skin. Gently, using tiny, tiny snips of the scissors, cut the matt out.

Yorkie Smarts

Teach your Yorkie to stand quietly as a training exercise. Ask your Yorkie to stand on the table, help him do it by using your hands to hold him, then praise him after a few seconds and give him a treat.

When the coat is free of matts and tangles, begin combing. Hold a section of the long coat between your fingers and comb the hair beginning at the last third of the length toward the ends of the hair. When the last third is free of tangles, comb the last two thirds of the coat, and then finally the entire length of that section. Comb the entire dog this way.

Watch Out!

Matts can pull skin tight, stretching it, so that when matts are trimmed out of the coat, the skin can be cut. Trim matts out very, very carefully, placing your fingers between the matt and the dog's skin.

It's often easier if you begin in a certain order. Many people find it easier to begin at the dog's head and work down the body. Personally, I like to begin at the ears. I get all the tangles away from the ears and work backward down the body, and I finish with the face. I don't know why this works for me, it just does. As you groom your dog, you will find what works best for you.

When the dog is combed out, run the pin brush through his coat. This will smooth it out and your dog will enjoy the massage of the brush. As you brush, you can part the coat so it lies correctly. Begin the part behind the dog's ears and run it down the dog's spine to the tip of the tail. The coat should lie flat on either side of the part. Sometimes a small squirt of hair spray will help it lie flat.

The Topknot

The topknot is made from the hair on the dog's forehead. By gathering the hair together and forming a small ponytail, the hair is kept out of the dog's eyes. To make the topknot, gather together all of the hair from the forehead. Divide the topknot from the beard at the invisible line from the corner of the dog's eye to the base of the ear. Hair above that line goes into the topknot and hair below that line goes into the beard.

With the hair gathered into one hand, smooth it by combing through it gently. Use a covered rubber band or hairband to hold the hair together. The placement of the topknot should be in the center of the head, equally between the ears and just slightly in front them. A barrette, with or without a bow, can be fastened over the rubber band.

Don't pull the hair too tight; that causes the dog to scratch at the topknot. Also, once each day, before you groom the dog, take the topknot down and massage the skin of the forehead. Rub all of the skin, making sure the blood is flowing well to the hair roots. This also feels good; when the hair is pulled one direction for a period of time, it can cause some mild discomfort and the massage will help alleviate that.

The Beard

The beard includes the hair under that invisible line from the corner of the eye to the base of the ear. It also includes the hair from the muzzle, including the hair from the top of the muzzle, which runs from the nose to the inside corner of the eyes.

The beard is high maintenance; more so than any other part of your Yorkie's grooming. The beard will pick up water every time your Yorkie takes a drink and will hold on to scraps of food after every meal. If your Yorkie goes hunting for mice in the backyard, the beard will drag in the dirt, picking up dirt and debris. In the house, it will find any dust bunnies you missed under the furniture!

Because of the beard's tendency to get dirty, it must be brushed daily. Begin combing from the bottom third of the hair as you did on the dog's body. When the bottom third of the hair is free of dirt and tangles, comb the last two thirds of the hair, and then the entire length of the beard. Part the hair in the center of the top of the muzzle from the nose to the middle between the dog's eyes. If brushing doesn't clean the beard, then you'll need to wash it.

The beard can grow quite long. In a conformation show dog, it can actually reach the floor! Most pet owners don't want to mess with this much beard, however, as it takes considerable maintenance. As your dog's coat grows, decide how much you are willing to maintain, and then keep the excess trimmed. Many Yorkie owners find a four- to six-inch beard fine. It's long enough to maintain the breed's expression but short enough to keep clean.

The Back End

Most groomers recommend trimming the hair around the anus to help keep the dog clean. If the coat is too long, feces can get caught in it, making a horrible mess. After your dog is thoroughly combed and brushed, use your scissors to very carefully trim the coat away from the anus. Just as when you trimmed matts, keep your fingers between the dog's skin and the scissors so that you don't cut the dog.

How much you trim is up to you. I suggest you trim just a little initially. After all, you can always trim more, but if you trim too much, you can't glue it back on (although it will grow back eventually). And if you trim too much, your dog could look really funny!

I also trim around my dog's genitals just to help keep things clean. For the boys, I trim the hair around the scrotum and penis sheath, especially at the head of the sheath. The hair on the end of the sheath can grow quite long and collect urine, looking horrible, smelling worse, and making the area susceptible to bacterial infections. For the girls, I trim the hair around the vulva.

Shampooing the Coat

Always comb out your Yorkie's coat thoroughly before bathing him. If you bathe him with tangles in the coat, those tangles will get worse. In fact, it will be as if you Super Glued them together! So thoroughly comb through the coat, getting out all of the tangles.

Yorkies are small enough to bathe in a sink, and that's usually the easiest place to do it. Leaning over a tub can be tough on the back, and they are too tiny to bathe outside under the hose! A rubber-backed bath matt on the bottom of the sink can help him keep his footing.

Before you put your Yorkie in the sink, have a couple of towels ready, plus both the shampoo and conditioner. Put a cotton ball in each of his ears to keep the water out, set the water to a nice comfortable temperature (test it on your wrist just as you would for a baby), and lift him into the sink. Use a calm voice to encourage him to be still, and try not to let him fight you.

Thoroughly wet him and then turn the water off. Work the shampoo into his coat, making sure to get the shampoo down to the skin. Rinse him off, working from his head to his tail and then underneath of him. Make sure all the soap is rinsed out. Then, work in the conditioner according to the manufacturer's directions and rinse it out.

When he is thoroughly rinsed, towel him off and wrap him in a towel for a few minutes. Cuddle him while the towel absorbs some more moisture and he warms up a little.

Blow Drying the Coat

Blow drying the coat serves a couple purposes. First, you can dry the coat while you brush it out, preventing any tangles from forming in the wet coat. In addition, you can keep your Yorkie from getting chilled while he's wet.

Unfortunately, many Yorkies don't like the hair dryer and fight it. It's important to introduce it to your Yorkie gradually and in a positive way. Bring out the hair dryer on a day when you have no intention of bathing your dog. Have a favorite dog toy at hand and a few dog treats. Sit on the floor with your dog and place the hair dryer on the floor, but don't turn it on. Ignore the hair dryer and encourage your dog to come close for the toy or treat. Play with your dog for a few minutes, letting him come close to the hair dryer, but while he does, don't touch the dryer. Just ignore it. Later, repeat these steps, but touch the dryer and move it. Continue this gradual introduction until you can turn the dryer on and let it blow toward him while you continue making a game out of the whole thing.

When your Yorkie will not panic with the blow dryer turned on him, you can then teach him to accept it while you dry him after a bath. With a couple towels under him, place him on the table where you groom him. Set the blow dryer on low and begin blowing the coat as you brush it with the pin brush. Blow and brush from the dog's body toward the end of the hairs. When the dog is entirely dry, finish him by brushing him all over, parting the coat and doing his topknot.

Grooming Challenges

If your Yorkie gets into oil, chewing gum, or gets sprayed by a skunk, a normal bath isn't going to solve the problem. Here are some suggestions for some special grooming challenges:

- **Burrs, foxtails and grass seeds.** These can often be picked out with your fingers or combed out with the metal comb. If they have caused a matt, a dab of hair conditioner or a drop or two of vegetable oil may ease them out. If the seed is in a bad matt, trim the whole thing (seed and matt) out.

- **Gum and other sticky stuff.** Use an ice cube to freeze it and break it out. If that doesn't work, use some hair conditioner or vegetable oil to ooze it out. If neither of these techniques work, trim it out.

- **Oil.** Joy dish soap will usually cut the oil. Just make sure you rinse the soap out thoroughly.

- **Paint.** Do not use paint solvents; they are toxic. Try to wash the paint out, and if that doesn't work, trim away the painted hair.

- **Skunks.** Tomato sauce rubbed into the coat and then washed out will help dull the smell. Several commercial products specifically for skunk smell are also available; check at your pet store.

Yorkie Smarts

If your Yorkie comes up with something original and unusual in his coat and you don't know how to handle it, call his groomer or veterinarian.

Touch Him!

One problem that many groomers complain about is that young dogs have not been taught to let people touch them all over. To make grooming easier for you and your groomer, make this a part of your daily routine. With your Yorkie on your lap, begin giving him a gentle massage. Start at his head and touch around his eyes, rubbing the lids gently, working down the muzzle to his mouth. Touch his nose. Open his mouth and touch his teeth and gums. Massage around his ears, down the neck to his shoulders and back. Continue in this way until you have massaged the entire dog, missing no parts of him.

This exercise will not only make it easier for you and your groomer to take care of your dog, but your veterinarian will love it, too. It's much easier to examine and treat a dog who is used to being handled than one who is leery of being touched.

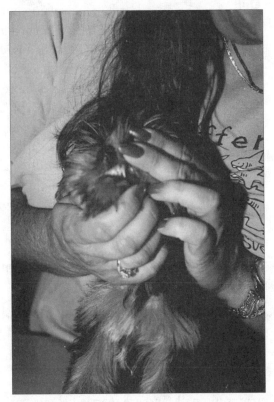

Teach your puppy to allow you to touch and clean his teeth.

Trimming Toenails

Trimming your Yorkie's toenails shouldn't be a stressful procedure, although many dogs turn it into one. If it's a part of your normal grooming, just as trimming your nails is a part of yours, you can eliminate a great deal of stress.

If you haven't bought a pair of toenail clippers, go ahead and get a pair. I prefer the kind that look like weird scissors with curved blades. You use them like scissors, too. I find these easy to use and the nail is very easy to see when trimming.

Watch Out!

If you hit the quick and the nail is bleeding, rub the nail along a bar of soap. The soap will clog the nail until a clot forms.

Yorkie Smarts

If your Yorkie is worried while you trim his nails, take a little peanut butter and pop it into his mouth to occupy him.

Have your Yorkie lie down in your lap or on your grooming table and take one paw in your hand. Pull the hairs back from around one toe and toenail. The nail is slightly curved over the quick but, once past the quick, becomes more slender and curves more sharply. You can see where the quick ends under the nail. The underside of the nail under the quick will be almost flat. Past the quick, the underside of the nail looks almost hollow.

Trim the nail slightly beyond the quick. If you cut into the quick it will hurt, your dog will cry, and the nail will bleed.

If your dog is very sensitive about his nails, just trim one paw at a time, take a break and do another paw later or the next day. Don't try to do all four paws and turn it into a raging battle. That will only make things worse.

If you hate trimming nails and are worried about hurting your dog, most groomers will trim nails for a very reasonable cost. If you have your groomer do it, however, make sure you visit regularly— every other week at a minimum—weekly is best. Nails grow very quickly and nails that are too long will hurt your Yorkie's feet.

Bet You Didn't Know

When your Yorkie is standing upright on all four paws, his nails should not touch the floor. You may hear them clicking when he's running but they should not touch the floor when he is standing still. If they do, they need to be trimmed.

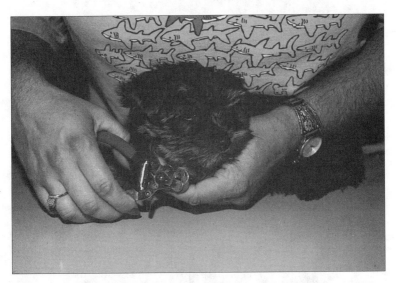

Keep toenail trimming sessions short and positive.

Ears, Teeth, and More

Besides keeping your Yorkie's coat tangle-free and clean and his nails trimmed, you'll also need to keep his ears and teeth clean and make sure his anal glands are expressed regularly. All of these are less than pleasant chores to some dog owners, but they are necessary and, once you make a habit of them, they really aren't as bad as they sound.

Cleaning the Ears

To clean the ears, you'll need a few cotton balls and some witch hazel or a commercial ear cleaning solution. Dampen a cotton ball, squeezing out most of the moisture, and while gently holding the ear flap, wipe the inside of the ear. Make sure to get into all the folds and creases. Don't try to go deep within the ear; just clean what is easily reachable. If the ear is dirty, use two or three cotton balls.

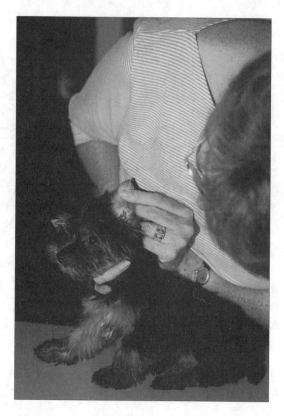

Check and clean ears regularly.

Cleaning Teeth

Dogs need their teeth cleaned just as we do. When the teeth are dirty, bacteria builds up and the mouth becomes diseased. A dirty mouth can also lead to other health problems. We know now that bacteria from a dirty mouth can affect the dog's heart, liver, and kidneys; sometimes quite seriously.

A child's toothbrush will work well for your Yorkie, along with toothpaste made specifically for dogs.

When you begin brushing your Yorkie's teeth, do so very gradually. Rub a few times on one spot in the mouth and then stop. Praise your dog, make a fuss over him, and then repeat it. Come back later and do some more. In the beginning, don't try to brush all of his teeth thoroughly. Instead, get him used to it gradually so he doesn't fight you.

Watch Out!

Don't use toothpaste made for people. Not all of the ingredients are safe for dogs and most dogs dislike the taste.

What Are Anal Glands?

The anal glands are small glands found on each side of the anus. As the dog relieves himself, small amounts of the oil produced in those glands are squeezed out with the feces. This oil is individual to each dog and is one reason why dogs smell each others' feces.

Sometimes, especially when stools are soft or when the glands produce too much oil, the glands become full. This causes pressure and irritation. Many dogs will at this point drag their rear on the ground, scratching the glands and trying to relieve the irritation. Unfortunately, this dragging can get dirt into the glands and cause even more irritation, sometimes to the point of serious infections.

Groomers often routinely express anal glands during grooming especially if a particular dog is known to have a problem. However, since many dogs express their glands normally, this should not be done unless your veterinarian recommends it. During your dog's next visit to

Bet You Didn't Know

If your dog is suddenly startled and produces a strong, offensive odor and you find a few dark brown oily spots, that is the oil from the anal glands.

the vet, or if your dog seems to have an irritated anus, ask about the anal glands. If your veterinarian seems to think it's warranted, he or she may show you how to check on the anal glands, and if needed, how to express them.

The Least You Need to Know

- The Yorkie's wonderful coat needs special care.

- If caring for the long coat is too much for you, a Yorkie with a hair cut is still an attractive dog and a wonderful pet.

- Grooming is a process and should be done regularly.

- Trimming toenails doesn't have to be stressful.

- Cleaning your Yorkie's ears, brushing his teeth, and checking his anal glands should be a part of your dog's regular grooming care.

Chapter 10

Keeping Your Yorkie Healthy

In This Chapter

- 🏠 Working with your veterinarian
- 🏠 Spaying and neutering
- 🏠 Taking care of your Yorkie
- 🏠 The importance and fun of exercise and playtime

Yorkies are, as a general rule, hardy, healthy little dogs. They can't maintain this good health by themselves, however. Your care is vital to their ongoing good health and so is your veterinarian's knowledge, help, and care. Between the two of you, you can help your Yorkie live a long, healthy, active life.

Your veterinarian will recommend that your Yorkie be spayed or neutered. He or she will also emphasize the importance of regular exercise. Both of these things are important to continued good health. But play is important, too, for both you and your Yorkie, and we'll talk about why.

Your Partner in Your Yorkies' Health

A veterinarian you trust will be a great help to you in maintaining your Yorkie's good health. Even long-time dog owners have questions about canine health, and your veterinarian is the person to ask.

Watch Out!

Make sure you read the breeder's, rescue group's, or shelter's contract carefully. Many require action of some kind should the puppy have a health problem. Make sure you know what to do.

Bet You Didn't Know

In the text, I refer to the veterinarian as a "he" for simplicity's sake—it's awkward to write or read "he or she." However, by doing so, I mean no disrespect to women veterinarians; they have my highest respect. In fact, more women are attending vet schools today than men!

Your neighbor, friend, or relative may offer help, but they may also give you incorrect or incomplete information. In Chapter 5, we discussed finding a vet and the importance of establishing yourself as a client. Now that your Yorkie is a part of the family, he needs to meet the vet, too.

Your veterinarian will want to examine your Yorkie within the first couple of days after you bring the dog home. Most breeders, rescue groups, and shelters request (and some require) that the dog be examined soon after purchase or adoption. This examination can assure you of the dog's good health or pinpoint any potential health problems. If your dog came with a health guarantee, this visit is a necessary part of the agreement.

During the exam, the vet will look the puppy over carefully, looking at his eyes, ears, teeth, skin, hair coat, and genitals. He will look at the outside of the puppy for outward problems and then will begin examining the puppy with his hands. He will feel for anything that is out of the ordinary or feels like a potential problem. He will watch the puppy as he moves his hands over the puppy's body to see if the puppy tenses or winces when touched. This could signal soreness from rough play, an injury, or an illness.

Your vet may also be looking for congenital problems. If the puppy has untreatable or potentially expensive health problems, or is genetically unhealthy, you have the right (if you so desire) to return the puppy to the breeder. If the puppy has a problem and you decide to keep him anyway, the breeder should be willing to give you a full or partial refund.

If you adopted your Yorkie from a rescue group or a shelter, there will probably be no health guarantee. However, if there are drastic health problems, you may decide to return the dog before you are too emotionally attached to him. If you decide to keep this Yorkie, even with health problems, knowing about those health problems right away can help you deal with them or prepare for them.

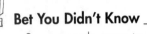

Bet You Didn't Know

Some people seem to resent the money spent at the veterinarian's office. However, your vet's goal is to keep your Yorkie healthy, and any money spent in preventive medicine is money well spent!

Vaccinations

A puppy from a breeder or a dog from a shelter or rescue has probably already received some vaccinations. If you have the vaccination records (try to get them if you don't) bring them with you to the vet's office. He will set up a vaccination schedule depending upon the vaccinations already given.

Vaccinations work by giving the dog an inactive form of the disease so the dog can develop the right antibodies (disease fighting cells) without the threat of getting sick. Most vaccines stimulate the body to produce antibodies for a period of time. Booster shots are then given to continue the protection.

Dog Talk

Vaccines are either modified live or killed. Modified live vaccines are considered more effective but do carry a small risk of transmitting disease.

Vaccinations are most often given for the following diseases (the diseases are described in detail in Chapter 12):

Rabies

Distemper

Parvovirus

Hepatitis

Leptospirosis

Coronavirus

Adenovirus

Parainfluenza

Bordatella

Lyme disease

Which Vaccines?

Your veterinarian will recommend a vaccination schedule depending upon where you live and which diseases are seen in your area. For example, if coronavirus isn't a problem in your region, your vet may not feel it's important to give your dog that vaccine. However, if you will be traveling to an area where coronavirus is common, you should mention that to your vet.

Potential Problems

Modern vaccines have saved millions of dogs' lives, but that doesn't mean vaccines are risk-free. Unfortunately, vaccinations do have some risks associated with them.

The most common side effect of a vaccination is a small, hard lump that forms at the injection site a few days after the injection. This is called a sterile abscess and needs no treatment; it will go away on its own.

Allergic reactions may also occur after a vaccination. Mild reactions may include shivering, a low-grade fever, or redness at the injection site. Some allergic reactions can be quite serious, however, including anaphylactic shock. Anaphylactic shock can be life threatening and always requires immediate veterinary care. Because of the dangers of an allergic reaction, always remain at the vet's office for at least 30 minutes after your dog has received a vaccination—even if you just sit in the waiting room—to make sure your dog isn't going to have a reaction.

Yorkie Smarts
You are responsible for your Yorkie's health and care, so don't hesitate to ask as many questions of your veterinarian as you wish. He shouldn't take offense by your questions. Just ask them nicely, of course!

Too Many Vaccinations?

Recent research has begun to question the wisdom of giving vaccination boosters every year, as has been the common practice. Many veterinarians, breeders, dog owners, and researchers are coming to believe that too many vaccinations—either at the same time or too close together—may be damaging dogs' immune systems.

Some veterinarians are now giving booster vaccinations every 18 months instead of every 12 months; and some veterinary schools are recommending that many boosters can be safely given every 36 months instead of 12!

Talk to your vet about the vaccination schedule he proposes. How close together is he scheduling shots? How many does he give at one time? Is he concerned about the frequency of booster shots?

Watch Out!
The dangers associated with vaccines doesn't mean you shouldn't have your dog vaccinated; the dangers caused by the diseases themselves are much, much greater!

Only the Healthy!

Your Yorkie should be vaccinated only when he is healthy. If he's not feeling well, he's at increased risk of getting sick from the vaccination itself, or his immune system may not respond well to the vaccination. In addition, the stress of the vaccination may make his original illness worse, depending, of course, upon what the original illness is.

Recognizing Problems

Your Yorkie should visit the veterinarian's office at least once per year even if he seems perfectly healthy to you. If your vet is giving vaccinations on an annual basis, this is the time to give those shots. However, if your vet is giving vaccinations on a different schedule, your Yorkie should still see the vet once per year. During these annual visits, your vet can evaluate your dog's health, see any changes from the previous year's visit, and hopefully catch any problems before they become a bigger problem.

However, because you see your dog every day, you are the best person to catch problems early. Pay attention to anything that changes in your dog's actions. For example, a lack of appetite may simply mean your dog is hot, and he may eat later in the evening when the weather is cooler, but a lack of appetite over several meals may signal something worse.

Call your veterinarian if you notice any of these potential problems:

- A temperature of lower than 100 degrees or higher than 102.5.

- Diarrhea that lasts more than one day, or that contains a significant amount of mucus or has blood in it.

- Vomiting that continues more than a couple hours.

- Loss of appetite for more than two meals.

- Distended abdomen and obvious tenderness.

🏠 Fainting, collapse, or seizures.

🏠 Potential allergic reactions, including swelling, hives, or rashes, especially around the face.

🏠 Respiratory distress, including coughing that won't stop, trouble breathing, or a suspected obstruction.

🏠 Potential poisonings, especially antifreeze, rodent poisons, snail poisons, insecticides, or herbicides.

🏠 Cuts or wounds that gape open or don't stop bleeding with direct pressure.

🏠 Suspected snake bites, bites from other wild animals, spiders, cats, and even other dogs.

🏠 A leg that is held up, with no weight put on it, and is obviously hurt.

🏠 Eye injuries—they are almost always emergencies.

Some things are not quite as obvious but could still signal trouble. Call your veterinarian for advice if you see any of the following:

🏠 Your Yorkie is hiding and won't come out.

🏠 Your Yorkie is panting when the weather and his activity levels don't warrant it.

🏠 Your Yorkie is restless for no apparent reason.

🏠 Your Yorkie refuses to participate in normal activities.

Watch Out!
Never ignore any of these warning signs in the hopes that they may go away. Waiting could be dangerous for your Yorkie.

Tell Your Vet Everything

When you call your veterinarian with a suspected problem, tell him everything. Don't assume that something may be too trivial or is unimportant. Instead, tell him everything you can possibly think of and let him worry about the significance of it. That's where his knowledge and experience come in.

In return, your vet will ask you some questions. Expect, at the minimum, these questions:

- What is the specific problem or the symptom that causes you to think there is a problem?

- What made you notice it?

- What are all the symptoms or the behaviors that are out of the ordinary?

- What is your dog's rectal temperature?

- Has he eaten? When and how much?

- Is there any vomiting? If so, what was vomited up?

- Is there diarrhea? When and how often? What does it look like? Is there mucus or blood in the feces?

- Has the dog been in contact with anything out of the ordinary? Did he get into the trash? Or have you been traveling?

- How long has this been going on?

Listen to Your Vet

When your veterinarian is talking to you, listen. Listen carefully and take notes if you want. Make sure you know what to do with your Yorkie. If he has prescribed medication, find out how much medication you should give and when. Make sure you know when the vet wants to see your dog again. Get all the information so that you can care for your dog as best you can.

Bet You Didn't Know

To give your Yorkie a pill, make a peanut butter sandwich—a tiny one. Take a small piece of bread, spread a little peanut butter on it, and fold it in half with the pill in the middle. Your Yorkie will gobble it down! Be sure that the medication can be given with food.

Spaying and Neutering Are Important!

Most female Yorkies should be spayed and males neutered. The only Yorkies who should be bred are those who are the best in physical conformation, temperament, and genetic health. By breeding only the best of the breed, you are helping to make sure that future puppies are even healthier than those of today, with fewer genetic defects and with good, sound temperaments.

Just because a particular Yorkie is a wonderful pet and well loved by all who live with him or her, it doesn't make that dog a good candidate for breeding. A well loved pet may not be of correct physical conformation as per the breed standard and may carry unknown genetic defects.

Breeding is a big job. To do it correctly, research must be conducted into the ancestors of the male and female being considered for breeding. Were the ancestors of these two dogs of correct physical conformation? Did any of their offspring produce any puppies with problems, emotionally or physically? Did any of their offspring have health problems? Did they live long, healthy lives?

Besides the research involved, the breeding process itself can be stressful. Sometimes the male will need help and often the female will not want to cooperate. Could you help if your dog doesn't want to be involved? It's not easy.

There can also be problems during pregnancy or before, during, and after birth. Tiny female Yorkies often need help during delivery.

The tiny puppies also occasionally need help to thrive. Are you ready to bottle raise a litter if the mother doesn't have any milk, or worse yet, just decides she wants nothing to do with the puppies? It happens!

Then what happens when those puppies need homes? If your dog is simply a well loved pet, with no championship, obedience, or agility titles to attest to her abilities, will anyone want your puppies? Don't count on that neighbor or friend who said they wanted one when your dog was a puppy; those people disappear quickly when puppies are actually available.

Unfortunately, many people breed their dogs, or allow their dogs to be bred, without knowing the realities of responsible dog breeding. The end result is hundreds of thousands of dogs born only to be killed in shelters. And yes, even Yorkies have been euthanized in shelters. As I write this today, there is a Yorkshire Terrier in each of the three local shelters within driving distance of my home. They will, unfortunately, remain there because the rescue groups are full and cannot take in anymore. There are too many people breeding Yorkies and too few homes available.

The thousands upon thousands of dogs who have ended up in shelters across the country cost taxpayers money. When these dogs are added to the dogs causing problems in communities, especially dog bite situations, dogs become more of a problem than a benefit.

Bet You Didn't Know

Every dog who is given up as unwanted costs taxpayers money.

Because of this, many cities and communities across the United States are trying to regulate dog breeding. Many have instituted fines or costly licenses to discourage dog breeding.

These measures may hamper or discourage the reputable, responsible breeder but unfortunately, they won't do anything to control indiscriminate, accidental breedings. However, a spayed or neutered dog cannot reproduce, even accidentally.

Traditionally, dogs have been spayed or neutered at about six months of age. However, many humane societies—in an effort to curtail breeding—have been spaying and neutering very young puppies, some as young as eight weeks of age. This has been very successful and has shown to have no ill effects on the puppy's health.

What Happens?

Spaying a female dog consists of a surgical ovariohysterectomy. The ovaries and uterus are removed through an incision in the abdomen. Your veterinarian will tell you to keep her quiet for a few days so she doesn't hurt herself, but most dogs show very few ill effects from the surgery. Most bounce back very quickly.

Yorkie Smarts
A female who has been spayed will no longer go through her two to three times per year "season." She will no longer spot on the floors and male dogs will no longer come "calling."

Male dogs are neutered (castrated), which consists of removing the testicles through an incision just in front of the scrotum. Again, your vet will tell you to keep him quiet for a few days. Most male puppies have very little pain afterward, usually acting as if nothing has happened.

Yorkie Smarts
Have you heard that a spayed or neutered dog will get fat? That's a myth. Dogs get fat when they are given too much food and not enough exercise!

Other Benefits

Spaying or neutering your Yorkie has a number of health and behavioral benefits besides simply stopping reproduction.

For the females, spaying ...

🐾 Decreases the incidences of mammary gland cancer.

🐾 Protects against cancers of the reproductive system.

🏠 Decreases the incidences of female aggression.

For the males, neutering ...

🏠 Decreases male sexual behaviors, including leg-lifting, marking, roaming, and fighting.

🏠 Decreases the urge to escape from the yard.

🏠 Protects him from testicular cancer.

Taking Care of Your Yorkie

Most of this book is focused on helping you care for your Yorkie in one way or another, so having a section titled, "Taking Care of Your Yorkie" may seem superfluous. However, let's take a look at some specific things that can help you care for your Yorkie as best you can. When you take reasonable care, and do so consciously, you are better equipped to keep your Yorkie as safe and healthy as possible.

Maintain Safety

Hopefully, you puppy-proofed your house and yard before you brought home your Yorkie, but have you kept it that way? It's very easy to forget to put things away, and some car repair chemicals, pool supplies, or fertilizer for the backyard could kill your Yorkie should he decide to get into it. It's important to maintain that puppy-proofing—that level of safety that we discussed before you brought your Yorkie home.

Yorkies are incredibly curious and will stick their noses into places where they have no right to be. They are this way because they were rodent hunters, and rodents hide in those places. Unfortunately, it can also get them into trouble. Look at life from your Yorkie's point of view. He is tiny, very low to the ground, and his viewpoint is very different from yours.

Yorkies are also incredibly athletic and can easily learn to climb obstacles. It only takes one exploration trip for a Yorkie to learn that if he climbs up on a hassock, he can then get on a chair, and from the back of the chair he can reach the bird cage. Using similar techniques, he can access cupboards or shelves that you probably thought were safe.

Being overly protective in this regard is not bad and, in fact, could save your dog's life.

Common Sense

Common sense also plays a big part in keeping your Yorkie safe. Don't let him explore the garage if it's not safe. Put child-proof locks on cupboard doors. Don't let him off leash outside of a fenced-in yard until he's grown up and very well trained and, even then, don't let him off leash near a street.

Common sense and reasonable care will go a long way toward keeping your Yorkie safe.

Get Out and Have Some Fun!

Yorkies are usually added to a family as a companion dog; most often a lap dog. They are usually companion dogs for adults, as other breeds make better companions for kids. What many people forget, though, is that Yorkies were not bred (originally) as lap dogs. Yorkies may be tiny and incredibly cute, but they are still terriers with an urge to do stuff, instincts to hunt, and a lot of natural athletic abilities.

Yorkies need to be active; they need to do things. They need to run and jump, to explore safe places, and smell new smells. Yorkies need

Watch Out!

Begin any exercise program slowly. Just like people, Yorkies can get sore muscles from doing new or strenuous activities.

activities that will keep their mind active and their body healthy. A Yorkie who lives his life on a lap without exercise, playtime, and mental stimulation will not thrive. He will get fat, lose muscle tone, and his mind will get dull. How sad!

Your Yorkie may be tiny but still needs daily exercise.

Exercise Ideas

One of the benefits of a tiny dog—as compared to larger breeds—is that exercise is much easier. It's tough to exercise a Great Dane in a small house, but very easy to exercise a Yorkie!

Exercise ideas for inside the house:

🏠 Play retrieving games by throwing a ball or toy across the room or down the hall.

🏠 Extend your foot or leg as you are sitting and teach your Yorkie to jump over it.

Exercise ideas for the backyard:

🏠 Play retrieving games.

🏠 Call him to come between two people, taking turns, and encouraging him to run as fast as he can back and forth a few times. Stop before he gets too tired or loses interest.

Exercise ideas outside:

🏠 Go for walks in different places.

🏠 Go for a hike in the local woods or meadow.

🏠 Go for a jog at the local park.

Bet You Didn't Know

It's important to remember that when you are simply walking, your Yorkie is running. Try to moderate your pace so he can keep up without getting exhausted.

It's Playtime!

Play is important to all sentient creatures, both young and old. Researchers have been telling us for years that play in the young is preparation for adulthood, but recent research has shown it's important for other reasons, too. Playtime helps animals bond with other members of their group. It builds relationships and makes them stronger. When two beings (human or other animals) play together, they feel something for each other and seem to be more likely to support one another.

Play between a dog and owner is very much the same. If you and your dog don't play together, the relationship lacks something that is hard to describe. The sense of fun and of pleasure isn't there; the sense of companionship isn't the same. However, when you play with your dog, the two of you can relax, laugh, enjoy each other's company, and simply have fun.

Playtime can be a part of exercise, especially if you play physical games such as retrieving games. But playtime can also be separate from exercise. Playtime also doesn't have to be anything formal; you don't have to do anything specific. Just sit on the floor, roll your Yorkie over, and rub his tummy as you talk silly to him. Let him bounce up and run circles around you as you pat the floor and threaten to catch him. Play can be, and at times certainly should be, silly.

Yorkie Smarts

Most dog trainers, myself included, usually tell dog owners not to wrestle and play tug of war with their dogs because it teaches the dog to use his strength against you. However, Yorkies are so small and you are so much bigger, it's usually not a problem. Go ahead and play!

That Special Bond

People get dogs for a variety of reasons. Some may want a protector and guardian, and feel safer with a dog's ears and instincts guarding them. Some people want a jogging companion and a playmate. Many people know that a dog is a social magnet! What dog owners know, though, even if only subconsciously, is that we feel more complete when we share our life with a dog (or two or three).

The bond that a dog and owner feel is one that happens with no other pets or animals. I have cats and love them very much, but I don't have the bond with them that I do with my dogs. Horse owners say the same thing; their horses are special, but the relationship isn't quite the same.

When a dog and owner have that bond, they feel responsible for each other. They watch and look out for each other. There is affection and love, but there is also respect.

That bond develops through time spent together. Exercise, playtime and laughter, companionship, and quiet times all work toward building that bond. There will not be a certain instant when you

A Yorkie's coat is traditionally long and flowing—even on his face!

There's no doubt about it—Yorkies are lap dogs!

A well-behaved Yorkie can be a good friend.

Yorkies participate in many sports, including agility.

Although Yorkies love to be held, they'll be healthier and happier if they get plenty of exercise.

Your Yorkie should meet friendly dogs of other breeds.

It's a good idea to spend time with Yorkies before deciding if one is right for you.

Yorkie owners treasure their tiny pets.

It's playtime!

Your Yorkie's crate shouldn't be too big.

A healthy Yorkie is bright-eyed, alert, and happy.

Tiny food treats can be wonderful motivators.

Go outside with your Yorkie.

Yorkies are tiny and cute and really, really easy to spoil!

will notice, "hey, we're bonded!" No, it develops more gradually than that. You'll know you've bonded with your dog when you find that you want to spend time with him; when he's not by your side you'll miss him. You know you're bonded when you worry when he's got a burr in his paw, or when he doesn't want to eat dinner. When you can't imagine life without him—you're bonded!

The Least You Need to Know

- Work with your veterinarian to keep your Yorkie healthy.

- Spaying and neutering will help avoid unwanted puppies, and offers other health and behavioral benefits.

- Common sense and reasonable care will help keep your Yorkie safe.

- Exercise and playtime are important for your Yorkie's continued good health and to help cement the bond between you both.

Chapter 11

Good Nutrition Is Important

In This Chapter

- 🏠 The ins and outs of canine nutrition
- 🏠 All about commercial dog foods
- 🏠 Cooking for your Yorkie
- 🏠 Taking a look at supplements
- 🏠 When to feed and how much

News reports bombard us daily with information about what foods are good for us and what foods are horrible. One week we may hear that a certain food will prevent cancer and the next week another report will say how unhealthy that same food is. When it's so hard to keep track of the foods we should eat, how can we figure out what our dogs should eat?

Luckily, feeding our dogs is a little easier; their natural diet is a little simpler than ours is. However, we still need to find out as much as we can about our dogs' nutritional needs so that we can provide them with the best diet possible for good health.

All About Canine Nutrition

Dogs are *carnivores*, just as their ancient ancestors and distant cousins, wolves, are. Carnivores eat meat, both by catching prey and by taking advantage of carrion (already dead prey). However, almost all canine carnivores are also known to eat fallen fruits, berries, and some tubers and roots. Although this might seem to make canines *omnivores*—animals that eat meats and plants—they are still officially classified as carnivores.

Dog Talk

An **herbivore** eats plants; a **carnivore** eats meat; and an **omnivore** eats plants and meat.

Your Yorkie needs a diet that supplies all of his nutritional needs. Good nutrition helps his body function as it should, maintains his health, and allows him to grow. Good nutrition also supplies him with energy for exercise and play. Good nutrition is made up of many things. Vitamins, minerals, proteins, amino acids, enzymes, fats, and carbohydrates are all necessary for good nutrition:

🐾 **Vitamins.** These organic compounds are necessary for life. Without them, food could not be digested, your dog could not grow, and there would be a total cessation of a thousand other bodily functions. Several vitamins, including A, D, E, and K are fat soluble, which means the body can store them in fat. Other vitamins, including all of the B complex vitamins and C, are water soluble. These are flushed out of the system daily in the urine and must be replenished through the foods consumed.

Yorkie Smarts

If you find your Yorkie eating dirt or chewing on rocks, he may be suffering from a mineral deficiency. Offer him a daily mineral supplement.

🐾 **Minerals.** These inorganic compounds are also necessary for life, although in much smaller amounts than vitamins. Necessary minerals include calcium, phosphorus, copper, iron, and potassium, as well as several others.

Minerals require a delicate balance for good health—some work only in the presence of others, and more of them isn't necessarily better.

🏠 **Protein.** Meat is good quality protein; either beef, chicken, lamb, fish, or any other meat. Proteins are found in other sources, too, including eggs, dairy products, and some plants. Complete proteins contain all of the amino acids necessary for good health. Incomplete proteins contain some, but not all, of the necessary amino acids. Good sources of complete proteins include eggs, red meats, fish, milk, and dairy products. Incomplete proteins, that are still good nutrition when combined with other proteins, include beans, peas, soybeans, peanuts, grains, and potatoes.

🏠 **Amino acids.** Amino acids are necessary for many body functions including growth and healing as well as for hormone, antibody, and enzyme production. When proteins are digested, they are broken down into amino acids, making them usable by the body. There are 22 known amino acids, and 12 of those are considered essential for canine life.

Bet You Didn't Know

The amino acids essential for canine life include arginine, citrulline, histidine, isoleucine, leucine, lysine, methionine, phenylalanine, taurine, threonine, tryptophan, and valine.

🏠 **Enzymes.** Enzymes are protein-based chemicals that cause biochemical reactions in the body and affect every stage of metabolism (the process of converting food to its chemical parts, which can then be used by the body). Some enzymes must work with a partner, a coenzyme that is often a vitamin, to cause the needed reaction or metabolism. Some enzymes are produced in the dog's body while others are found in the food the dog eats.

🐾 **Fats.** Fats are a necessary part of good nutrition, especially for growing puppies and active dogs. Fats are needed to metabolize the fat-soluble vitamins and to supply energy for activity. Fats may be found in animal meats and in plant based oils.

Bet You Didn't Know

Some dogs who are fed foods that are high in carbohydrates (especially carbohydrates from cereal grains) will show symptoms of hyperactivity. These symptoms often disappear when the dog is fed a food lower in cereal grain carbohydrates.

🐾 **Carbohydrates.** Carbohydrates are sugars and starches found in plants. Carbohydrates are fuel for the body. Your Yorkie's body runs on carbohydrates like your car runs on gasoline. Complex carbohydrates (potatoes, pasta, peas, grains, and rice) are intricate conglomerations of glucose (sugar) molecules.

Commercial Dog Foods

Commercial dog foods are designed to supply all of your Yorkie's needs, including proteins, amino acids, enzymes, fats, carbohydrates, vitamins, and minerals. However, all dog foods are not created equal—when it comes to dog food, you usually do get what you pay for. In most cases, the more expensive dog foods are better foods than the less expensive foods.

What makes one dog food better than another can be based on many things. How and whether the food is tested during development can be used in considering if it's a quality product. Testing may consist of *feeding trials* and, in fact, many of the larger companies, Iams for example, maintain large kennels for feeding trials. In some feeding trial kennels generations of dogs have been fed only those specific diets. But feeding trials are not the only means of testing the foods; some companies use laboratory testing to determine the nutritional value of a food. However, laboratory testing doesn't necessarily prove that a dog will thrive on the food. Foods that are tested by actually feeding dogs (feeding trials) will say so on the label of the dog food, or you can call the company that makes the food. There should be a phone number on the label.

The quality of a dog food is also based on the quality of the ingredients. Grains grown in mineral-poor soils will have few minerals to pass on to the dog who consumes them. Poor quality meats will be less nourishing for the dog. Less expensive foods typically contain inexpensive and less nourishing grains and less of the more expensive, but more nutritionally satisfying, meats. Again, the dog's nutrition can, and often will, suffer when he is fed low quality foods.

Dog Talk

Feeding trials are tests in which certain numbers of dogs in a controlled environment, such as a kennel, are fed a specific food for a specific period of time. The dogs' health is analyzed during and after the trials.

Many dog owners are also concerned about many of the preservatives, artificial flavorings, and additives in a lot of dog foods. Some of these additives are of questionable nutritional value. If you are concerned about a particular additive or ingredient, call your veterinarian and call the manufacturer of the food. Find out what they say about that ingredient.

Bet You Didn't Know

Yorkies suffering from poor nutrition will have a dry or dull coat, flaky skin, brittle nails, and will be more lethargic than normal.

Reading the Label

The label on each bag (or can) of dog food will tell you a lot about that particular food. One section of the label lists the percentages of nutrients. Most Yorkies will thrive on a food that contains about 28 percent protein and 8 percent fat, although if your Yorkie is older and tends to gain weight a slightly lower percentage of fat is fine.

The label will also tell you the ingredients of the food. Ingredients are listed in order of amounts contained. Therefore if beef is listed first, followed by rice, corn, and wheat you'll know that there is more beef in the food than there is rice and there is more rice than corn. This can be deceptive, though. For example, if you have a dog food label that lists the ingredients like this: beef, wheat bran,

Yorkie Smarts

Although Yorkies aren't as prone to major allergies as are some other toy or terrier breeds, some suffer from food allergies. If you have an allergic Yorkie, reading the ingredients on the dog food label is very important.

wheat germ, and wheat midlings; does that mean there is more beef than wheat? No, it doesn't. It means only that there is more beef than wheat bran; and more beef than wheat germ. However, if all of the wheat ingredients were added together, there could very easily be much more wheat than beef.

Are Preservatives Safe?

Preservatives are added to commercial dog food to keep it from spoiling. Unfortunately, not all preservatives are created equal. The most controversial preservative currently used in dog foods is ethoxyquin, a chemical that prevents the fats in foods from becoming rancid and the vitamins from losing their potency. Ethoxyquin is approved by the Food and Drug Administration for use in human foods but it has come under criticism from the general public. It has been alleged that ethoxyquin causes cancer, kidney, liver, and thyroid problems. However, none of these claims have been proven.

If you are concerned about ethoxyquin or any other chemical preservatives, look for a food preserved with tocopherols. These antioxidants are naturally occurring compounds of vitamins C and E. Just be aware that tocopherols have a very short shelf life; make sure to check the expiration date on the food.

Different Forms of Food

Dog foods are found in four basic forms: dry kibble, canned, semi-moist, and fresh foods (which may also be frozen).

Dry, kibbled foods come in a bag and usually contain grains and meats. Dry foods have a good shelf life and most dogs eat them quite readily. They are usually very affordable; some more so than others.

Canned foods are mostly meats (chunks or slices of meats) or meat recipes (processed meats with other ingredients). These foods have a high moisture content. In the can they have a long shelf life, but once the can is opened they must be used right away. Canned foods are very palatable to dogs and are much more expensive than dry foods.

Semi-moist foods have a higher moisture content than dry kibble foods but not as high as canned foods. These foods are very high in sugar and salt as well as artificial colorings. The ingredients can also vary significantly, so it's even more important to read the label carefully. Many treats are semi-moist in formulation.

Fresh foods have become quite popular in the past few years. These foods are usually meat recipes (meats combined with other ingredients, usually vegetables but not cereals). Fresh foods are very difficult to preserve without adding preservatives; the shelf life is a matter of days. Therefore, most of these foods are preserved by freezing, although some are de-hydrated.

Some dog owners prefer to feed human foods to their dogs, cooking for them on a daily basis, while others have decided to feed a diet based on raw (uncooked) foods.

Bet You Didn't Know

Nutrition is a very complex subject, and I could write a book on reading the labels and selecting the right food for your dog. In fact, I did! It's called *The Consumer's Guide to Dog Food* (Howell Book House, 1996).

What kind of food should you feed your Yorkie? Because Yorkies eat so little—especially when compared to larger dogs—the choice of what to feed them is very important. A good quality dry kibble food is fine for most Yorkies. Chewing the kibbles helps keep the teeth clean. Some tiny Yorkies have trouble chewing dry kibbles, though, and for these Yorkies a softer diet may be necessary. You can soak the dry kibble to make it softer, or you may decide to feed him softer foods. Ultimately, the choice of what to feed your Yorkie is yours.

Choosing the Right Food

Here are some suggestions to help you choose the right food for your Yorkie:

- Tiny dogs sometimes have trouble chewing dry kibble. Is that a problem? If it is, you need to crush the kibble, soak it to soften it, or feed him softer foods.

- Take a good look at the list of ingredients on the dog food label. Are you comfortable with your dog eating those ingredients?

- What are the protein and fat percentages? Most Yorkies will thrive on a diet of 28 percent protein and 8 percent fat.

- How active is your Yorkie? If you are training for competitive obedience and agility, you may need to feed him a food higher in calories. Perhaps a food with slightly higher percentages of protein and fat, but not too much.

- If you have any questions about the food, talk to your veterinarian and call the food manufacturer.

After your dog has been eating the food for four to six weeks, evaluate the results. This is the food's final test, and will help you decide whether or not you have chosen the right food for your dog. Answer the following questions:

🏠 How is your dog's weight? Is he too skinny? Is he too fat? You should be able to feel ribs (with a little flesh over them) but not see them.

🏠 How is your Yorkie's coat? It should be shiny and soft with no oily feel and no doggy odor.

🏠 What is your Yorkie's energy level like? Does he have enough energy for work and play? Does he have too much energy? Does he seem hyperactive? He should have plenty of energy for work and play without bouncing off the walls!

🏠 Does he act starved or always hungry? Often dogs whose bodies are missing vital nutrients will chew on everything and will act starved even though they are eating regularly.

Cooking for Your Yorkie

I cook for one of my dogs. She is eight years old and is suffering from liver disease. Since an incorrect diet can add stress to the liver, I have been cooking for her for several years with my veterinarian's approval. In fact, he has asked me to share my "doggy liver diet" with some of his other clients. And as I write this, Dax is still doing well. (Knock on wood!)

Cooking for your dog can be a lot of work. It is certainly more work than scooping some dry kibble out of the bag! But cooking for your dog requires thought, too, because it can be quite difficult to formulate a home cooked diet that meets all of your dog's nutritional needs. Yorkies present a special challenge, too, because they are so tiny. With a stomach the size of a small walnut, Yorkies get full very quickly. You have to make sure they get all of the nutrition they need in that walnut-size meal!

The key to making a homemade diet work is using a variety of ingredients to make sure the dog is receiving all of the necessary amino acids and enzymes, as well as his required vitamins and minerals.

Basic Home Cooked Maintenance Diet

The following recipe is a home cooked maintenance diet for dogs with no known food allergies. The amount fed each day will vary depending upon your Yorkie's weight, weight loss or weight gain, activity level, and energy needs. Most Yorkies should be offered approximately $1/3$ to $1/2$ cup of the finished food per meal (figuring on two meals per day). Increase or decrease it from there as your dog loses or gains weight.

Mix well together in a big bowl:

1 lb. cooked ground meat (chicken, turkey, or lamb) drained of most of the fat

2 cups cooked whole grain brown rice

$1/2$ cup cooked, mashed barley

$1/2$ cup oatmeal, cooked

$1/2$ cup raw grated carrots

$1/2$ cup finely chopped raw green vegetables (no lettuce)

2 TB. olive oil

2 TB. minced or mashed garlic

Divide into meal sized servings (usually $1/3$ to $1/2$ cup) and store in the freezer. Thaw one day's serving at a time.

When serving, add the following:

1 tsp. yogurt with live active cultures

1 multi-vitamin/mineral dog *supplement*

Tiny pinch of kelp

Yorkie Smarts

A **supplement** is anything that is added to the dog's diet. It may be a commercial supplement, an herbal remedy, or other foods.

Bet You Didn't Know

One downfall to home cooked diets is their effect on your Yorkie's teeth. Dry kibble foods scrape the teeth as they are chewed, helping to keep the teeth clean. If you feed a homemade diet to your Yorkie, you'll have to work harder to keep his teeth clean.

The Pregnant or Lactating Mother Dog's Home Cooked Diet

This home cooked diet is for pregnant or lactating bitches.

Mix together in a large bowl:

1 lb. ground meat, cooked, do not drain off the fat

4 large hardboiled eggs, shelled, crumbled

1 cup cooked whole grain brown rice

1 cup cooked oatmeal

1 large sweet potato, cooked, mashed

$1/4$ cup wheat germ (as long as dog is not allergic to wheat)

$1/2$ cup grated raw carrot

$1/2$ cup finely chopped green vegetables

2 TB. olive oil

2 TB. minced or mashed garlic

Store in refrigerator in a covered bowl or divide into individual servings and freeze; thaw servings one day at a time. Servings may need to be larger as the pregnancy progresses.

When serving, add the following:

1 tsp. yogurt with live active cultures

Dash dry powdered milk

Dash brewer's yeast

Pinch kelp

1 vitamin/mineral dog supplement

Hypoallergenic Diet

This diet is for dogs allergic to meats and/or grains and grain products.

Mix together in a large bowl:

5 large potatoes (russet or sweet potatoes or a combination of both), cooked and mashed

3 eggs hardboiled, shelled, crumbled

1 cup finely chopped or grated green vegetables

1 cup cooked beans (not green beans), finely chopped or mashed

$\frac{1}{2}$ cup grated carrot

2 TB. olive oil

1 TB. minced garlic

Store in covered bowl in refrigerator or divide into individual servings and freeze.

Add when serving:

1 teaspoon yogurt with live active cultures

1 vitamin/mineral supplement

Pinch kelp

Changing Foods

Most Yorkies have a pretty sturdy digestive system. Unlike many other breeds, changes don't seem to bother Yorkies too much. However, when changing foods, do so gradually so that you don't cause gastrointestinal upset. When changing from one dry food brand to another, or when changing the types of foods, add the new food very gradually to the old, taking about three weeks to make a complete change. If your Yorkie seems to have an upset stomach, diarrhea, or doesn't want to eat, you may be making the change too quickly.

Taking a Look at Supplements and Treats

Do you take vitamins? You probably feel better about your own overall diet and nutritional health when you do. For the same reason, many dog owners feel better about their dog's nutritional well-being when they add a vitamin/mineral supplement to the diet.

Supplements don't have to be in pill form, however. A supplement is anything that is added to the basic diet, and that can include some herbal remedies as well as foods with special nutritional qualities. A supplement can make the difference between good nutrition and better nutrition.

Some supplements that can add to your Yorkie's better nutrition and that will not cause a nutritional imbalance might include:

🐾 **Yogurt.** A good nutritious food on its own and a good source of protein, amino acids, and fat. Yogurt with live active cultures adds beneficial bacteria to the digestive tract. Add no more than one teaspoon per day for a Yorkie.

🐾 **Brewer's yeast.** Excellent source of B vitamins and minerals, including the essential trace minerals chromium and selenium; a good nutritious food on its own. A dash or a pinch per meal is fine for Yorkies.

🐾 **Eggs.** Cooked only (raw egg yolks interfere with vitamin B absorption and have been associated with salmonella poisonings) are excellent sources of proteins, a variety of vitamins, minerals, and amino acids. Cook one egg and split it up between several meals.

Watch Out!

Too much supplementation can upset the nutritional balance of the previously balanced commercial food. Supplement carefully and wisely. When in doubt, talk to your veterinarian, the dog food company, and the makers of the supplement, and then balance all of their recommendations.

🏠 **Kelp.** A good source of iodine, calcium, potassium, and other minerals and essential trace elements. Use according to manufacturer's directions; usually a pinch is plenty.

When adding supplements to your Yorkie's food, make sure you add small amounts so that the total of supplements will not add up to more than 10 percent of the dog's daily diet. Any more than this could upset the nutritional balance of the commercial food.

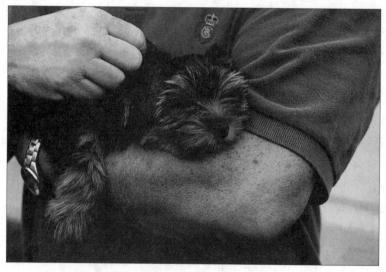

Tiny dogs should eat at least two meals per day.

When to Feed and How Much?

Tiny Yorkie puppies should eat at least twice per day and may even prefer to have four small meals per day. Follow your puppy's needs. However, try to feed at set times. Don't offer food every time your puppy acts hungry. He needs a schedule—especially for housetraining!

Adult Yorkies will do well with two meals per day, in the morning and evening.

Yorkies Don't Eat Much!

Your Yorkie does not need much food. As you saw in the section on home cooked meals, $^1/_3$ to $^1/_2$ cup is a large Yorkie-size serving of that food. Many Yorkies will need even less. With any food—commercial dry kibble, canned food, or even a home cooked diet—you can tell how much to feed by watching your Yorkie. If he gains extra weight, cut back a little on the amount you're feeding him. If he begins to lose weight when he shouldn't, feed him a little more.

Although commercial dog foods will state on the label how much food you should feed your dog, that is simply a guideline. All dogs—even those of the same breed—have individual needs. One dog could eat $^1/_3$ cup, maintain his weight well, and have plenty of energy while another gains weight on the same amount.

The Least You Need to Know

- You get what you pay for with dog foods; and generally, the more expensive foods are better quality.

- Dog food labels will tell you a lot about the food, including ingredients, nutritional value, and the preservatives used.

- Healthy homemade diets are possible; but take care with your ingredients and watch your dog closely to monitor the results.

- Most Yorkies will do well when fed twice a day, although puppies may need to eat more often.

Chapter 12

Health Problems to Watch Out For

In This Chapter

- Making sense of health problems
- Small dogs have special problems
- Dangerous diseases
- Fleas, ticks, and other bugs

This chapter covers some of the less appealing aspects of dog ownership. After all, no one wants to know that their beloved Yorkie might have a serious health problem. However, knowledge is a good thing, and we'll just hope you never need to use it!

This chapter will discuss some of the health problems Yorkies can face, including the special problems tiny dogs can have. We'll also talk about those nasty parasites all dogs can pick up and what you can do about them.

Inherited Health Problems and Birth Defects

Genetic health problems are inherited from the puppy's ancestors. Either the mother or father had the gene causing the problem, or both had the genes, or one or both were carriers of the gene. Research has been ongoing and will probably continue for many years as to how genetic diseases are passed, but many questions remain to be answered.

Congenital health threats (often called birth defects) are present at birth but may or may not be hereditary. Identifying which health problems are genetic or congenital is also the subject of much study.

Dog Talk

Genetic health prob-lems are inherited. **Congenital health threats** are present at birth but may or may not be inherited.

For example, my now eight-year-old dog, Dax, has a liver disease, and we now know she has had it since she was a puppy. As far as we have been able to determine, it was not inherited, but we don't know that for sure.

The Nervous System

Although epilepsy and other seizure disorders are not common in Yorkies, they are not unheard of. Seizures may be as mild as a "freezing," where the dog doesn't or can't move, to a grand mal seizure with strong convulsions. Experts now believe that most seizure disorders are inherited, although this has yet to be proven. Seizures can also be caused by exposure to toxins or even by other diseases.

If your Yorkie has a seizure, make him comfortable and don't allow him to hurt himself, but don't try to stop the seizure. After the seizure, he'll be groggy and disorientated for a little while. Take him to the veterinarian's office as soon as possible after the seizure; blood tests can often pinpoint the cause of the seizure.

The Internal Organs

Some Yorkies have been found to have a developmental defect involving the blood supply and the liver. During fetal development, blood bypasses the liver. However, shortly after birth, this bypass should close, allowing the blood to go through the liver so that the liver can remove toxins and wastes from the blood. When the bypass does not close, the blood is not cleansed and gradually the dog sickens. This condition, called portosystemic liver shunt, or portacaval shunt, can sometimes be corrected with surgery. It usually shows up in fairly young dogs—under six years of age and often younger. Puppies with this condition do not thrive, do not gain weight, and sometimes have seizures.

Yorkies have also been known to have Cushing's disease, also known as hyperadrenocorticism. In this disease, the adrenal glands produce excess hormones, causing many different symptoms and problems including poor muscle tone, nervous system disorders, hair loss, excess thirst and urination, and high blood pressure. The condition tends to show up in older dogs. If you notice any of these symptoms, talk to your vet immediately.

The Eyes

Yorkies have fewer problems with their eyes than many other breeds. Older dogs may develop cataracts, although this is more of an aging problem than a congenital or genetic problem. Occasionally some Yorkies have dry eyes, a problem that is usually related to the tear glands and ducts. Dry eyes require veterinary care, so if your Yorkie rubs his eyes a lot, blinks, squints, or keeps his eyes closed, see your veterinarian right away. If the eyes are not treated immediately, the corneas can become scarred, causing permanent damage.

The Skin

Yorkies can be allergic to many things, including grass, pollen, dust mites, and flea bites. The skin usually appears red, sometimes with bug bites apparent, but not always. Your Yorkie will also scratch a lot and chew on himself. Some dogs itch so badly they mutilate themselves, so this is not something to ignore. Dogs suffering with skin allergies are miserable. See your vet right away so that you can stop the allergic reaction, and then you need to try and figure out what's causing the problem.

The Skeletal System

The most common skeletal problem seen in the breed is luxated patellas. In this disorder, the kneecap (patella) is not held in place properly, causing the dog to hop and skip until it moves back into place. The extent of the disorder may range from very mild—when the dog just skips once in a while—to more severe—with the dog holding a leg up and crying in pain. Depending upon the extent of the problem, your vet may recommend corrective surgery.

Legg-Calve-Perthes Disease is also seen in Yorkies. In this disease, a poor blood supply to the head of the femur (thighbone) causes the bone to deteriorate. First symptoms appear in late puppyhood and may show up simply as limping. As the disease progresses, symptoms worsen until no weight is put on the leg at all. Surgery is usually recommended.

Bet You Didn't Know

The Orthopedic Foundation for Animals (OFA) and PennHIP maintain lists of dogs who have been x-rayed for hip and elbow dysplasia. Breeders can then research the lists and eliminate from their breeding plan any dog who is or has produced dogs with questionable elbows and/or hips.

Hip dysplasia is a deformity of the hip joint. The dog may show lameness and may not want to move. Although this is more common in larger breeds, it is, unfortunately, being seen in more and more small dogs and has been seen in Yorkies. Although surgery is sometimes an option, with tiny dogs such as Yorkies, sometimes veterinary management is recommended rather than surgery. Talk to your vet about options.

Elbow dysplasia is a deformity of the elbow, much like hip dysplasia, and will show up as lameness and a lack of desire to move. This is not common in Yorkies but has been seen in the breed.

Small Dogs Have Special Problems

Their very size makes small dogs susceptible to some special problems. Obviously, small dogs are more fragile, and if stepped on or inadvertently kicked, may suffer from broken bones or internal injuries. Many tiny Yorkies have been hurt when they were asleep on a chair or sofa and someone accidentally sat on them! Accidents will happen, unfortunately, but take care to prevent as many as possible.

Watch Out!

Get into the habit of looking for your Yorkie. Look where you step and look before you sit down.

Many toy breeds, including Yorkies, suffer from hypoglycemia (low blood sugar). In dogs suffering from hypoglycemia, when blood sugar levels drop too far, the dogs will become weak, drowsy, disoriented, and if it progresses, the dog can have a seizure or go into a coma. This is most common in puppies, and many will grow out of it. It is most commonly seen in the very tiny Yorkies (under 4 to 5 pounds when full grown). The condition requires veterinary assistance and management.

It is not uncommon to hear tiny dogs, including Yorkies, coughing. Sometimes the cough is caused by the dog pulling on the leash. When the leash puts pressure on the trachea, the trachea may give, bend, or even partially collapse, causing the dog to cough or even gasp for air. If the dog has a weak trachea, even hard breathing during play or exercise could cause a partial trachea collapse, again causing coughing or gasping. If this happens, the veterinarian should be consulted for possible treatments.

Dangerous Canine Diseases

We talked briefly about these diseases in Chapter 10 while discussing vaccinations. Here is a little more information about them.

Rabies

The rabies virus is carried by infected wildlife and is highly contagious. It is transmitted in the salvia, either through a break in the skin or by a bite. It is always fatal.

Watch Out!

Never allow your Yorkie to play with a wild animal, especially one that's acting strangely. Bats, skunks, and raccoons have been known to carry rabies.

Fortunately, vaccines have been very effective in preventing the disease. Rabies vaccines are required by law throughout the United States and proof of vaccination is required prior to obtaining a dog license.

Distemper

This is a contagious viral disease. Dogs with distemper have a fever, are weak, depressed, have a discharge from the eyes and nose, cough, vomit, and have diarrhea. Many will show neurological symptoms, including staggering and lack of coordination. The virus is passed through the saliva, urine, and feces. Most infected dogs die.

The distemper vaccination usually prevents the disease; however, vaccines work by stimulating the immune system. If the immune system is threatened or if the puppy does not receive the complete series of vaccines, he may not be adequately protected.

Parvovirus

Commonly called parvo, parvovirus is a terrible killer of puppies. It attacks the inner lining of the intestines, causing bloody diarrhea.

This diarrhea has a very distinctive smell that veterinarians and breeders who have dealt with the disease quickly learn to recognize. In young puppies, the disease also attacks the heart, causing death, often with no other symptoms. The virus replicates very quickly, and dehydration can lead to shock and death within a matter of hours.

The vaccination for parvo is usually effective, although this virus has been known to mutate, rending the vaccine useless. The vaccine is often given in conjunction with other vaccines, but many vets and breeders feel that it should be given alone for the best results.

Infectious Canine Hepatitis

Infectious canine hepatitis is another highly contagious viral disease. It primarily attacks the liver but can also damage the kidneys. It is not related to the human forms of hepatitis. The virus is spread through the saliva, mucus, urine, and feces. Initial symptoms include depression, vomiting, abdominal pain, fever, and jaundice.

Mild cases can be treated, but the mortality rate is very high. Vaccinations can prevent this disease.

Coronavirus

Coronavirus is rarely fatal for adult dogs but can be very dangerous for puppies. Symptoms include vomiting and loose, watery diarrhea. The virus is shed in the stools. Dehydration from the diarrhea and vomiting is the primary danger for puppies. Vaccinations can prevent this virus.

Leptospirosis

Leptospirosis is caused by bacteria, not a virus, and is passed in the urine. The bacteria attack the kidneys, causing kidney failure. Symptoms include fever, loss of appetite, possible diarrhea, and jaundice. Antibiotics can sometimes treat the disease but some dogs die, primarily due to the tremendous damage the bacteria cause.

The vaccinations can usually prevent the disease although leptospirosis can appear in different forms (serovars) and the vaccine may not protect against all forms. Care must be taken to not spread this highly contagious disease; it can spread to people and other dogs.

Kennel Cough

Tracheobronchitis, adenovirus, and parainfluenza are a few of the diseases commonly referred to as kennel cough or canine cough. All three of these cause significant coughing, sometimes with a fever, sometimes without. Most healthy adult dogs can recuperate from these without veterinary care; however, young puppies and older dogs need careful monitoring, as a secondary respiratory infection can occur. In some cases, pneumonia develops.

Bet You Didn't Know

Kennel Cough got its name because when one dog in a kennel situation begins coughing, it usually spreads throughout the kennel.

Vaccinations usually prevent these diseases; however, viruses can and do mutate and often well vaccinated dogs will still come down with some form of kennel cough. Kennel cough can be best compared to a human cold; we don't know what exactly causes either of them and, in fact, the causes may be numerous.

Fleas, Ticks, and Other Bugs!

External parasites—fleas, ticks, and mites—are insects that are uniquely suited to pester your dog. Fleas, ticks, and mites have a long history of destruction behind them, too. Fleas have been blamed for innumerable plagues throughout history, including the bubonic plague that decimated Europe many years ago. Today these are still pests and can still threaten your dog's comfort and health, although we have a much better arsenal at our fingertips to combat them.

Fleas

A flea is a small, slightly crescent-shaped, six-legged insect with a big abdomen and a small head. It's a tremendous jumper and is flat sided, so it can slip through hair with ease. When caught, it will pop under (or between) your fingernails like a tiny balloon. If that sounds gross, you obviously haven't dealt with too many fleas! Fleas cause dogs so much torment, it can be very satisfying to pop the little pests!

Fleas live by biting your dog, taking a drop or two of blood each time they bite. A heavy infestation can actually cause anemia from the blood loss in Yorkies. Many dogs are so allergic to flea bites, the poor dogs will scratch, dig, and chew themselves raw. An allergic dog could end up with flea bite dermatitis or open sores, which could then develop into secondary infections.

Bet You Didn't Know

To check for fleas, place your Yorkie on a solid-colored sheet. Brush his coat thoroughly then let him up. If you see salt and pepper type residue, your dog has fleas. The residue is fecal matter (the "pepper") and eggs (the "salt").

Fleas are also the intermediate host for tapeworms, which will be discussed later in this chapter. If your dog has fleas and, during chewing, swallows a tapeworm-infected flea, the dog can then become infested with tapeworms. Fleas can also carry diseases, including bubonic plague. Obviously then, these pests are more than simply annoying to you and your dog; they are also a very real health threat.

Fortunately, in the past few years several products have been introduced to make flea control easier and safer. In past years, insecticides and pesticides were the only available products, and you had to use those with caution. If you weren't careful, you could easily end up poisoning yourself and your dog before you killed off all the fleas.

Some new options include:

- **Systemic topical treatments.** These products are applied to the skin, usually between the shoulder blades, and the product is absorbed into the dog's system. Depending upon the product, the flea is killed when it bites the dog or its reproductive cycle is disrupted.

- **Systemic products.** Your dog swallows a pill, which transmits a chemical throughout the body. When the flea bites the dog, it picks up this chemical. The chemical prevents the flea's eggs from developing and hence, the insect population dies off.

- **Insect growth regulators (IGRs).** These products stop the immature flea from developing or maturing, thus preventing it from reproducing.

To control fleas you must hit them in three ways: on the dog, in your house, and in your yard. Leave out any one of the three, and your control efforts will fail. If you have found fleas on your dog, then you can be sure that you have them in the house and in the yard, because the fleas are on your dog only to feed; they do not live on the dog. They live in your house and yard!

Watch Out!
Always read the directions on all flea control products. Make sure you use them correctly to keep your dog and your family safe.

Some control methods might include the following:

- **In the yard.** Use a spray designed for outside use that contains an IGR. Repeat as recommended.

- **In the house.** Use a spray for inside use with an IGR. If your house is infested, use a spray with a quick kill ingredient as well as an IGR. Use according to directions.

- **On the dog.** Use a systemic product such as Program or Sentinel. Do not use insecticides or flea collars in addition to the systemic product unless the label on both products specifies that it is safe to do so.

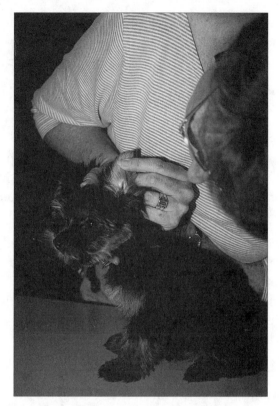

Fleas can seriously threaten a tiny dog's health, so check for them often during flea season.

Ticks

Ticks are eight-legged, oblong insects with a head that embeds into the skin. Ticks feed on the host's blood and, when engorged, will drop off. Ticks, like fleas, are carriers of human and canine diseases. In the United States, they carry Rocky Mountain Spotted Fever, Lyme disease, as well as other diseases. Rocky Mountain Spotted Fever is an acutely infectious disease that is characterized by muscular pains, high fevers, and skin eruptions. Lyme disease, which affects dogs as well as people, causes a lingering fever and joint pain (sometimes quite severe) and can also cause neurological problems.

Although some flea products are partially effective on ticks, they are rarely totally effective at killing or keeping ticks off your dog.

Yorkie Smarts

Ask your veterinarian if Lyme disease is a problem in your area. If so, find out if he recommends giving the Lyme disease vaccination.

During tick season (spring and summer) you will have to examine your dog daily and remove each and every tick. Check your dog all over, but pay especially close attention to ticks' favorite spots: behind or in the ears, in the armpit area of the front legs, and around the neck.

Never remove a tick with your bare fingers. Use tweezers or wear rubber gloves. Grab down close to the skin and pull gently but firmly, with a slow twisting motion. Don't flush the tick; it will survive its trip downstream and live to bite again or worse yet, reproduce! Instead burn it to kill it. Put a little antibiotic ointment on the wound where the tick was embedded.

Mange Mites

Mange is usually associated with stray dogs who have no one to care for them. This isn't necessarily so. Many well-loved dogs have come down with mange one way or another.

Mange is caused by mites—tiny microscopic pests—that live on the dog. Your veterinarian will do a skin scraping to look at under the microscope to see if mites are present. Mange comes in two varieties:

- **Sarcoptic mange** is contagious to people and other pets. Its primary symptoms include red welts, and the dog will be scratching continuously. Sarcoptic mange usually responds well to treatment.

- **Demodectic mange** is not considered contagious and shows up with bald patches, usually first on the dog's face, and there may not be any scratching or itching. Demodectic mange often appears in young dogs and will clear up with treatment. However, in older dogs, treatment can be long and drawn out and is sometimes not effective at all.

Watch Out!

Suspected mange mite infestations should always be seen by a veterinarian for diagnosis and treatment.

Ringworm

Ringworm isn't really a worm at all but instead is a very contagious fungus that infests the skin and causes ring shaped (round) scaly, itchy spots. These round spots are the trademark identification of ringworm. It is spread by contact; perhaps from another dog, a cat, or even a wild animal.

Ringworm usually responds well to treatment, but care must be taken to follow the treatment plan according to directions as set up by your veterinarian because this is very, very contagious to people and other pets.

Ickk! Bugs Inside!

Internal parasites are just as disgusting as external parasites but can be more threatening to your dog's health because they are not as easily seen. You will see fleas on your dog, for example, but your dog could have internal parasites for quite a while before you notice any signs of poor health.

Most internal parasites can be detected by taking a small piece of your dog's stool to the veterinarian's office. The stool will be prepared and then examined under a microscope. Parasites, the eggs, or larvae can then be detected, and your vet can prescribe appropriate treatment. After treatment, your vet will ask you to bring in another stool sample—usually in two to three weeks—to make sure the treatment was effective. Parasites that dogs are susceptible to include:

🏠 **Heartworms.** Heartworms live in the upper heart and greater pulmonary arteries, damaging the blood vessel walls. Poor circulation results, which in turn damages other body functions. Eventually, the heart fails and the dog dies. The adult worms produce thousands of tiny worms known as microfilaria. These circulate throughout the bloodstream until they are picked up by mosquitoes; the intermediate host. The microfilaria continue to develop in the mosquito, then, when they're ready, they can be transferred to another dog when that mosquito bites it. Preventive medications are available, easy to administer, and very effective. Talk to your veterinarian about heartworm preventives and whether heartworm has been found in your area. If heartworm is present, your vet will recommend a blood test to make sure your Yorkie has not already been infected. If the blood sample comes back okay, your vet will prescribe preventive medication.

🏠 **Roundworms.** These long, white worms are fairly common in puppies, although they can also be found in adult dogs and humans, as well as other animals. A dog with roundworms will not thrive and will appear thin, with a dull coat and a pot belly.

Watch Out!

Roundworm eggs can be picked up via the feces, your Yorkie should be discouraged from sniffing other dogs' feces.

Often you will see worms in the stool or vomit. Roundworms can be detected by your veterinarian through a fecal analysis. Good sanitation is important to prevent an infestation; feces should be picked up and disposed of daily.

🏠 **Hookworms.** Hoorkworms live in the small intestine where they attach to the intestinal wall and suck blood. When they detach and move to a new location, the old wound continues to bleed for a period of time, causing bloody diarrhea, which is often a symptom of a hookworm infestation. Hookworm eggs are passed through the feces and are picked up from the stools, as with roundworms. The eggs can be detected in a fecal analysis. Treatment often needs to be repeated two or more times before finally ridding the dog of the parasites. Good sanitation is necessary to prevent a re-infestation. Hookworms can also be spread to people.

Tapeworms. Tapeworms live in the intestinal tract and attach to the wall to absorb nutrients. They grow by creating new segments. Usually the first sign of an infestation is small rice-like segments found around the dog's rectum or in its stool. Tapeworms are acquired when the dog eats an infected flea, the intermediate host, or catches and eats rodents like mice, which can be hosts. Your vet can prescribe treatment but a good flea control program is the best way to prevent future tapeworm infestations.

Whipworms. Whipworms live in the large intestine, where they feed on blood. The eggs are passed in the feces and can live in the soil for a long time—years, even. A dog who eats the fresh spring grass or buries his bone in the infected soil can pick up eggs. Heavy infestations can cause diarrhea, and the dog will appear thin and anemic, with a poor coat. Whipworms are not as easily detected through fecal analysis as other worms, as they don't shed eggs in the stool as frequently as do round-worms and hookworms. Several stool samples may need to be checked to be certain. If caught early, your vet can prescribe treatment but heavy infestations can be fatal.

Watch Out!

If your dog has had whipworms, talk to your vet about treating your yard, since whipworm eggs can live in the soil for years.

Giardiasis. The parasitic protozoa, giardia, is common in wild animals. If you and your dog go camping or hiking and take a drink from a clear mountain stream, you can both pick up giardia. Diarrhea and lethargy are the

Yorkie Smarts

Take a sample of your Yorkie's feces to your veterinarian at least twice per year unless your vet requests it more often.

primary symptoms. Your veterinarian can test for giardia and prescribe treatment.

🏠 **Coccidiosis.** Coccidiosis is another parasitic protozoa, but this one is often carried by birds and rabbits. Symptoms include coughing, runny nose, eye discharge, or diarrhea. It can be diagnosed through a fecal analysis and your vet can prescribe treatment.

The Least You Need to Know

🏠 As a general rule, Yorkies are healthy, although they can be affected by some genetic or congenital health problems.

🏠 Vaccinations can prevent most of the diseases that threaten your Yorkie.

🏠 Fleas and ticks are more than just pests; they can make your dog sick!

🏠 Internal parasites are nasty and can threaten your dog's health.

Chapter 13

Emergency First Aid

In This Chapter

- 🏠 Knowing where to get help
- 🏠 Putting together an emergency first-aid kit
- 🏠 Restraining your Yorkie
- 🏠 Emergency first-aid guidance

I put together my first emergency first-aid kit almost 20 years ago. I was working at a veterinary hospital and saw a number of dogs come in, hurt, who had not even received basic first-aid care. In many situations, their owners could have saved their pets additional stress and harm simply by performing some basic first aid. I decided then that I would always have a first-aid kit available and I would know how to use the items in it. Since then, I've used my kit for myself and my husband, my own dogs, dogs belonging to friends and family, and even nieces and nephews! Friends and family make fun of my first-aid kit—a big red fishing tackle box—but they also know it's available and never hesitate to use it!

Emergencies do happen, unfortunately, and the best thing you can do is be prepared. Know what your veterinarian's emergency procedures are; have a credit card or cash ready; and know some basic first-aid techniques. Someday your dog's life could depend upon it.

Know Where to Get Help

Some veterinarians don't handle after-hours emergencies; they refer their clients to emergency animal hospitals. Other vets take all calls no matter what the hour of day or night. Neither policy is right or wrong as long as you understand the policy and know whom to call when that *emergency* happens and have clear directions as to where to go.

Before an emergency occurs, ask your vet or the emergency animal clinic the following questions:

- **Where is the clinic located?** Can you find it easily? Make sure you can find it even when you might not be thinking clearly.

- **What are your policies regarding payment for emergency care?** Many require complete payment upon services. If that's so, can you pay it? What happens if an emergency happens between pay days? Some dog owners have gone to the trouble of obtaining a credit card (usually MasterCard or Visa because they're accepted just about anywhere) and they have saved that card for emergencies. That way it's never overextended and it's available for emergencies. If you have pet health insurance, make sure it covers emergencies and that the clinic will accept it.

- **Do you have the facilities to keep dogs overnight? Does someone stay with the dog if it remains overnight?** Many times this depends upon the situation, so ask for clarification for your own peace of mind.

- **If the dog spends the night, what happens during business hours?** Many emergency clinics are closed during business hours so what will happen then? Will you be required to transport your dog to your veterinarian? Will the clinic do that?

🐾 **Will the clinic forward the emergency information to my vet or should my vet call the clinic?** Or will you hand carry the records with your dog?

Yorkie Smarts

Don't wait until there is an emergency to find out what your vet's policies are. Ask now so you know.

Make sure your veterinarian's phone number and the number of the local emergency animal clinic are readily available. Post them on the refrigerator, put them in your first-aid kit, and in your wallet. Sometimes it's hard to think clearly in an emergency so make things as easy for yourself as possible.

Dog Talk

An **emergency** is considered to be a potentially life-threatening injury or illness; or a health threat that should not wait until the next day.

An Emergency First-Aid Kit

As I mentioned previously, I use a large fishing tackle box to hold all my supplies—I like how big it is and that it has a lot of little sections and boxes to hold small items. On the outside I have written in very large letters "First-Aid Kit." I want it to be easily seen so if I send someone to my van who doesn't know what the kit looks like, he or she can easily spot it.

Some supplies I keep in my kit—and suggest you keep in yours—include:

🐾 Large and small tweezers

🐾 Round ended scissors and pointed sharp scissors

🐾 Disposable razors

🐾 Small nail clippers (for small dogs or cats)

🐾 Thermometer (rectal)

- Safety pins
- Mirror
- Pen and pencil
- Paper for notes and directions
- Tape of various sizes, widths, and types
- Butterfly adhesive bandages
- Rolls of gauze or fabric of different widths
- Gauze pads of different sizes, including eye pads
- Elastic wrap around bandages
- Instant cold compresses
- Antiseptic cleansing wipes
- Sterile saline eye wash
- Alcohol prep pads
- A small bottle of hydrogen peroxide
- Benadryl tablets
- Bactine
- Bacitracin ointment
- Kaopectate tablets or liquid
- A leash and collar

I also keep a gallon jug of water in my van, a dog bowl, and an old but sturdy sheet that can be used as a stretcher.

You'll need to check this kit often, to replace materials that have been used and materials or medications that have expired. Most medications do have an expiration date; don't use them after that date.

If you don't know how to use these materials, consider enrolling in a first-aid class. The Red Cross offers a first-aid course for dog owners in many regions of the country. If that's not available in your area, veterinarians can often be convinced to teach a class for a dog club or group for a minimal charge.

Bet You Didn't Know

The Red Cross offers a class in canine first aid and CPR. Call the local branch of the Red Cross to find a course near you.

Restraining Your Yorkie

Hurt dogs often panic. They thrash, fight restraint, and bite, claw, or scratch at anyone who tries to touch them. Many dog owners are unpleasantly surprised when their wonderful, beloved dog bites them after an injury. An injured dog isn't thinking clearly and is concerned only with getting away from the hurt. You, then, need to know how to restrain your Yorkie so that he can be prevented from hurting himself more than he already has, and so that you can protect yourself.

Prevent Him from Biting

The first thing you need to learn how to do is to muzzle him. By closing his mouth, gently but firmly, you can make sure he doesn't bite anyone when he's afraid or hurt. Granted, Yorkies are very small, but they can bite quite hard when they want to and a hurt Yorkie can definitely hurt someone.

You can make a muzzle out of just about anything that is long and pliable. A leash works very well, as does a bandanna or a length of gauze from your first-aid kit. Take the length of leash or material and wrap it quickly around your dog's muzzle at least two times. Wrap it gently—a Yorkie's muzzle is very small—but firmly. Then pull the ends back behind your dog's ears and tie it behind the neck. If you gently pull on the material around the muzzle it shouldn't slip off.

Watch Out!
Never muzzle a dog who is having trouble breathing!

Practice this on your Yorkie every once in a while. He won't like it, but that's okay. When you muzzle him, tell him what a good dog he is and when you take the muzzle off, give him a doggy treat to make up for the unpleasantness of it all!

Even a tiny dog can bite when afraid or hurt so be careful in those situations.

Be Still in Your Arms

One of the nicest benefits to having a tiny dog is that it's much easier to restrain them in an emergency. A hurt Great Dane is tough to control; your Yorkie can be held in your arms!

Practice by picking up your Yorkie and rolling him over on his back so that he is resting on one of your forearms, his head toward the inside of your elbow. Your hand of that arm can cup his hips and his body can be cradled in your arm up against your body. Your other hand can rest on his chest, controlling him so that he doesn't thrash or fight you.

In this position, you can see his face and he can see yours—which should be calming for him. You can also look at him, examining him for injuries. When he calms, you can take the hand off his chest to help examine him through his coat.

Practice this position every once in a while so he doesn't resist it when you need to use it. When you do this, practice examining him in this position, too. Touch his paws, look at his ears and teeth, and run your free hand through his coat. Let him get used to the whole examination. This way in an emergency it won't be something completely new to him.

Canine CPR

Cardiopulmonary resuscitation (CPR) is a vital first-aid skill. I will never forget the day my husband Paul and I came upon a dog who had been hit by a car. There were only minor injuries apparent; however, the dog wasn't breathing. We began CPR and within a few minutes the dog began breathing again. After a trip to the emergency animal clinic and treatment (there were some internal injuries), the dog made a full recovery. For years afterward, every time we saw that dog, Paul and I felt good about our efforts.

With Yorkies, CPR is slightly different than for larger dogs because of their tiny size. First of all, when you see a Yorkie lying still, you will want to make a quick evaluation prior to doing anything. Take the following steps:

1. Lift the dog carefully, moving him as little as possible (in case of other injuries), to a table, bench, or chair.

2. Check whether there is a heartbeat by placing two fingertips under either armpit.

3. Check whether he's breathing. Watch for his chest to move, or wet a fingertip and place it in front of his nose. His breath can be felt on your wet fingertip.

4. If he's not breathing, clear his mouth of any obstructions.

Watch Out! _____
When doing CPR, you must compress the chest enough to move the blood in the heart, yet not so hard as to break your Yorkie's ribs! Perform the CPR firmly yet gently.

Watch Out! _____
Don't practice CPR on a dog who isn't in a life-threatening situation. You could hurt him! Practice on a stuffed toy.

5. Pull the tongue out and to the side of his mouth so that it doesn't block the airway.

6. Close his mouth and pull his lips over the teeth to help make his mouth airtight. Cup your hand around his lips and muzzle.

7. Inhale a breath, and then exhale gently but firmly a small breath (a puff) into the dog's nose. Watch his chest for it to rise after you blow.

8. Repeat every five seconds if you can do so without hyperventilating yourself.

9. After 10 breaths, stop and do some chest compressions. Place him on his side, and using two fingers, compress the chest (very gently but enough to compress it slightly) five times. Then go back to giving him breaths. Do 10 breaths, then five chest compressions, then repeat the process.

Once you start CPR, continue it until your dog begins breathing again, until you can get your dog to help, or until it seems very obvious that it is in vain. But don't stop too soon, many dogs have been saved by canine CPR.

Emergency First-Aid Guidelines

In an emergency situation, it's important to be able to think and react quickly. If your Yorkie is bleeding, in shock, or overheating, your quick reactions could mean the difference between life or death.

The emergency guidelines listed in the rest of this chapter are not given to replace veterinary care. Instead, they are to aid you in caring for your Yorkie until you can get him to appropriate emergency care.

Bleeding

Bleeding occurs after just about any injury. How it should be treated depends upon the type of bleeding and its severity. If the skin isn't broken, there may be bleeding under the skin. This can result in a bruise if the injury is small. A bruise can be treated with an ice pack. Use the ice pack on and off at 15-minute intervals until it seems that the bleeding under the skin has stopped.

Bet You Didn't Know
A small bag of frozen vegetables makes a great ice pack.

Bleeding from small scrapes, scratches, and small cuts is usually not a danger. Wipe it off, apply pressure with a gauze pad if it's still oozing, and when the bleeding stops, gently wash it with soap and water.

Internal bleeding is very dangerous and less obvious. If your Yorkie has been in some kind of a rough accident—especially if he has been kicked or dropped— watch his behavior. If he stops moving, acts restless, or cries, get him to the vet's office right away. Other symptoms of internal bleeding include pale gums, a distended

Watch Out!
Yorkies are tiny and blood loss can quickly lead to shock or cardiac arrest.

abdomen, bloody diarrhea, bloody vomit, blood in the saliva, or coughed up blood.

A continuous oozing type of bleeding is also serious. You will need to put pressure on the wound, using layers of gauze pads and pressure from your hand, and you'll want to get the dog to your veterinarian right away. Stitches will probably be required.

Shock

A dog (like a person) will go into shock after a traumatic injury or during a serious, sudden illness. Shock is life-threatening and, when combined with what caused the shock in the first place, your dog could be in serious danger of dying.

Symptoms of shock include:

🐾 A rise in heart rate, often irregular

🐾 Panting or very rapid breathing; often gasping

🐾 Dilated pupils; a staring, glazed look to the eyes; pale gums; and no response to movement

You cannot treat your Yorkie for shock, other than keeping him warm, keeping him still, and getting him to a veterinarian right away. This is not the time to watch the dog and hope he'll come out of it on his own; he needs help right away!

Watch Out!
Never leave your dog alone in the car. The air inside a car heats up very quickly, even on cool days, and your dog could die of heatstroke before you return.

Heatstroke

A dog who is overheating will lay down, often flopping himself down, or will pace back and forth in agitation. He will be panting heavily and may go into shock. His body temperature will rise rapidly. You will need to immediately cool him down. Immerse him in cool water or pack him in ice and immediately get him to the vet's office.

Poisons

Symptoms of poisoning can vary depending upon what caused it. Some of the more common symptoms include extreme salivation and drooling, vomiting, diarrhea, and muscle tremors. The puppy's eyes may be dilated or he may suffer seizures.

In all situations where you suspect your Yorkie may be poisoned, call your veterinarian. Listed below are some of the more common household substances that are harmful to your puppy and what you should do if your puppy gets into them:

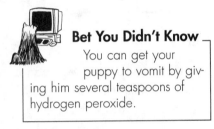

Bet You Didn't Know
You can get your puppy to vomit by giving him several teaspoons of hydrogen peroxide.

🏠 **Antifreeze.** Induce vomiting and get your puppy to the vet's office right away.

🏠 **Bleach.** Call your vet right away. He may ask you to induce vomiting or may recommend your bring your Yorkie to his office immediately.

🏠 **Chocolate.** This is poisonous to dogs so make him vomit and then call your vet.

🏠 **Gasoline.** Give him some vegetable oil to block absorption and take him to the vet's office right away.

🏠 **Ibuprofen.** Make him vomit and get him to the vet's office right away.

🏠 **Insecticides.** If ingested, get him to the vet right away. Do not induce vomiting unless your vet recommends it. If there was skin contact, wash him thoroughly.

🏠 **Rat, mouse, roach, or snail poisons.** Induce vomiting and get him to your vet's office right away.

Yorkie Smarts

The National Poison Control Center 24-hour poison hotline is 1-900-680-0000. No credit card is needed; your phone bill will be charged.

Bring with you to your vet's office whatever it was your Yorkie got into. If at all possible, bring the label with the name of the product and any ingredients. The more information you can give your vet, the better.

Burns

Burns can happen in a variety of ways. Thermal burns are those caused by heat, such as if your dog gets too close to a candle. Electrical burns can occur when the dog chews on an electrical cord. Chemical burns are the result of contact with a corrosive substance that causes a burn, such as bleach, gasoline, liquid drain cleaners, paint thinners, or road salt.

If you suspect your Yorkie has been burned, follow these directions:

1. If the burn is chemical in nature, rinse your Yorkie thoroughly. Treat it also as a potential poisoning.

2. Put an ice pack on the spot.

3. If the burn is not severe and the skin is simply red, keep it clean and watch it carefully to make sure it doesn't get infected.

4. If the burn is blistered, bleeding, and oozing or has damaged any layers of skin, take your Yorkie to the vet's office right away.

Insect Bites and Stings

If you suspect your dog has been stung or bitten by an insect, first try to find where on your dog's body the bite or sting happened. If there is a stinger, scrape it out. Don't grab it and pull it; that will squeeze more venom into your dog's skin. Scrape it out with a fingernail.

If you need to, shave away some of the dog's hair so you can see the sting or bite. Wash the area off, pour some hydrogen peroxide on it, and watch it. Some signs of allergic reaction include the following:

- Swelling at the site of the bite or sting and in the body tissues surrounding it
- Redness or extreme whiteness
- Fever
- Muscle ache, joint pain, and lameness
- Vomiting and/or diarrhea
- Difficulty breathing

If your dog is showing any of these allergic reactions, call your veterinarian right away. Your vet may recommend that you give your dog a Benadryl antihistamine immediately to combat some of the allergic reaction. He will also want to see your Yorkie as soon as you can bring him in.

Animal Bites

If your Yorkie is bitten by another small dog during playtime and the bite is a simple puncture, don't be too worried. Simply wash the bite and watch it. If it looks red and possibly infected, call your veterinarian. Check with the owner of the other dog to make sure the dog is well vaccinated, including for rabies.

However, if your Yorkie is attacked by a much larger dog, or an unknown dog, call your vet immediately, as this could pose a serious health threat. If you can, try to find the dog's owner to make sure the dog is vaccinated, especially with an up-to-date rabies vaccine.

Some bites may need special treatment, including antibiotics, drains, or stitches, to make sure they heal properly. There is also the danger that a larger dog could have caused internal injuries to your Yorkie.

Watch Out!

Wild animals carrying the rabies virus are not that uncommon. Skunks, raccoons, bats, and foxes have all been known to carry it. The best prevention is to make sure your Yorkie is vaccinated.

If your dog is bitten by a cat or a wild animal, you must get him to the veterinarian's office right away. Cat bites must be cleaned thoroughly right away as infections afterward are very common. Bites from wild animals must also be treated, and there is the very real danger of rabies.

Snake Bite

If your Yorkie is bitten by a nonvenomous snake, wash the wound with hydrogen peroxide or chlorhexidine and watch it to make sure the wound doesn't get infected.

If your Yorkie is bitten by a venomous snake, don't panic. First of all, many snakes do not automatically inject venom; the snake may strike to scare away your dog without actually injecting venom.

If venom is injected, your dog will begin to swell. If he was bitten on the leg, the leg will swell. Unfortunately, most dogs are bitten on the face because they stick their nose down into the snake's space and *whap!* the snake gets the dog on the nose or muzzle. If the nose or muzzle begins to swell, the dog is in great danger of suffocating, so get him to the veterinarian's office right away. Call ahead so the vet can begin making arrangements immediately to get the anti-venom. Take a good look at the snake so you can describe it to your vet; not all snakes are venomous.

While getting him to the vet's office, you need to stay calm so you can keep your dog calm. Keep him quiet, too, because limited movement will aid in slowing down the spread of the venom in his system.

Natural (and Other) Disasters

Where do you live? In southern California, we must deal with wild fires and earthquakes. In the Midwest, dog owners must put up with tornadoes. Family members in Florida must be able to survive hurricanes. Natural disasters—no matter where you live—are a fact of life, and you need to make preparations so that you can take care of your Yorkie as well as your family.

I keep my canine first-aid kit (which is combined with human first-aid supplies) easily accessible. When on vacation or a trip, the first-aid kit is in my van. I also have on hand a gallon jug of water; more when we're traveling in the desert. Extra leashes and collars are always in my van as well as in the first-aid kit.

Yorkie Smarts

My dogs always wear a buckle collar with a identification tag with my name and phone number on it as well as their license tag. My dogs are also tattooed and microchipped for identification.

In my garage, within reach of the side door, I keep an emergency kit in case of earthquakes or fires. It has some canned dog food that will keep a long time, a can opener, water, a smaller first-aid kit, and a variety of other supplies that are recommended for people.

A few of my neighbors think I'm either a little neurotic or overly concerned, but my husband and I have lived in this area for many years and twice have been evacuated due to wild fires. When ordered to evacuate, you don't have any time to put stuff together. You grab what you can and leave. My emergency kit has come in handy for both of those situations and it's there for any future emergencies.

Think about emergencies you may have to face in your region. If you live in a cold climate, make sure there are blankets and chemical hand warmers in your emergency kit. In a hot region you may want some extra water.

The Least You Need to Know

- Know where to get help in an emergency; both from your veterinarian and the local emergency animal clinic.

- Know how to restrain your Yorkie in an emergency so you can keep him from harm and protect yourself.

- Put together a first-aid kit, keep it stocked and handy.

- Know what to do in an emergency.

Part 4

The Well-Behaved Yorkie

Yorkies are very intelligent dogs, and they quickly learn how to manipulate their owners. Those big, dark eyes are so expressive, and when combined with a little wiggle of the body, most owners just melt and give in to whatever their Yorkie wants. Unfortunately, a spoiled Yorkie is rarely a good companion. A spoiled Yorkie is, instead, a pain in the, hmmmmm, neck!

A trained Yorkie is, however, a joy to spend time with! A trained Yorkie is happy, well behaved, and can have fun with his owner. A trained Yorkie is welcome places where the spoiled Yorkies will not be welcome. The trained Yorkie can travel, can participate in dog activities and dog sports, and can volunteer as a therapy dog. The joys and rewards of training are numerous and make all your efforts worthwhile.

There's a lot to learn, so keep reading!

Chapter 14

You Are Your Yorkie's Teacher

In This Chapter

- 🏠 The benefits of training
- 🏠 Training techniques and tools
- 🏠 Teaching your Yorkie
- 🏠 Being your Yorkie's leader
- 🏠 Tips to make your training more successful

Each year, thousands of dogs are given up by their owners because of problem behaviors. Perhaps the dog dashed out the front door and then wouldn't come back when the owner called. Maybe the dog had one too many housetraining accidents. Unfortunately, many of these dogs given up for bad behavior will never be adopted; they will be destroyed at the local shelter.

If you think this doesn't happen to Yorkies, you are mistaken. It does happen and it happens all too often. Yorkie puppies are very tiny and incredibly cute. They are very easy to spoil, and far too many Yorkie puppy owners do spoil them. However, a spoiled puppy is cute; a dog who carries those bad puppy habits into adulthood is not nearly as cute. Bad habits get old real quick.

Training You and Your Yorkie

Dog training is something you and your family and your Yorkie do together; it's something that you all participate in. During the training your dog will be learning new things, and so will you. You may have to change some of your ideas about dog ownership as well the way you do things around the house. Dog training should really be called "dog and owner training."

My dogs enjoy their training sessions, and your dogs should, too. A lot of dog owners make the mistake of thinking of training as military boot camp; instead, you should think of it as a new way of doing things. Training can also be fun. Teaching your dog tricks is great fun, and it's still teaching your Yorkie to do things for you, which is a big part of what training is all about!

Yorkie Smarts

Good dog training rewards desired actions of behaviors and discourages or ignores unwanted actions.

The benefits of training your Yorkie depend partly on your goals. However, even if you never plan on showing your Yorkie or competing in obedience trials, the benefits far outweigh the alternatives:

- 🏠 A trained Yorkie is housetrained in his own house and in others'.

- 🏠 A trained Yorkie won't dash out through open doors or gates.

- 🏠 A trained Yorkie is respectful of the house and the family's belongings.

- 🏠 A trained Yorkie is not a pest or nuisance and doesn't try to be the center of attention all the time.

🏠 A trained Yorkie and owner share a bond of mutual respect. Both understand each other's strengths and weaknesses.

🏠 A trained Yorkie looks up to his owner as his leader.

🏠 A trained Yorkie and owner can do more. A trained dog can be trusted off leash to play because he will come when his owner calls him.

Bet You Didn't Know
When you have trained your dog, you will find a bond of communication. He's so attuned to you it's almost like your dog can read your mind.

🏠 A trained Yorkie is fun to spend time with because he understands social rules and acceptable behavior.

Training Techniques and Tools

Every dog trainer has his or her own preferred method of training dogs. As long as the method is humane and effective, there is no right or wrong way. In this and the next few chapters, I will be introducing you to the techniques that I have been developing and using for the past 20 years in my dog training classes.

My training techniques are called balanced training. I use a balance of *positive reinforcements* or techniques to reward the dog for doing something right and *negative reinforcements* (corrections) for discouraging behavior we don't want to happen again. The primary emphasis is on the positive, but we also let the dog know when he's made a mistake.

Dog Talk
A positive reinforcement is something the dog likes, such as food treats, a toy, petting, and verbal praise.

I use these techniques in my classes as well as with my own dogs. I use exactly the same techniques when raising one of my puppies. By watching my dogs, my students can then see what is possible with the training if they persist and follow through with it. Not only that, my students (and you, the reader) can see that I have enough faith in what I am teaching you to use it with my own dogs.

A group training class is excellent socialization and teaches your dog to work around distractions.

Dog Talk

A correction or **negative reinforcement** is something that gets the dog's attention as he makes a mistake, such as saying "No!" or snapping and releasing the leash.

Some trainers prefer to use positive techniques that call for the owner to ignore bad behavior. If this technique works for your Yorkie, awesome! I have found, though, that many Yorkies are too smart for a technique like this and will continue bad behavior simply for its own sake. For example, if your Yorkie likes to bark when the mailman delivers the mail, barking (and the mailman leaving) becomes self-rewarding. Ignoring the bad behavior will not stop it. You may try and distract him when the mailman arrives, but in most cases, the reward of barking is too strong. In balanced training, not only would you try and distract your dog, but if he ignores you and barks anyway, you would then let him know he's made a mistake.

It's important that you find a technique that is comfortable for you because you need to participate in this process and believe in it. If you're ambivalent about it, you won't be successful.

Bet You Didn't Know

Learning is an ongoing process. Every time you interact with your Yorkie, you teach him something, and it may (or may not) be what you want him to know! Think about it—what are you teaching him right now?

Books, Videos, Classes, Private Training: Which One?

This book gives you a good description of how to teach your Yorkie the basic commands. Plus, we'll discuss a number of the more commonly seen behavior problems. Is this going to be enough? For many Yorkies and their owners, yes, it will. Yorkies who are basically good dogs and owners who have been able to establish a good relationship with their dogs may need only basic obedience training.

Other Yorkies (and their owners) may need more help. Group classes provide socialization opportunities and a lot of distractions. Some dogs need this stimulation while others need to learn to ignore the disruptions. Group classes are particularly good for puppies who need socialization.

Private training is quieter and allows the instructor to tailor the instruction individually for each dog and owner. Some owners need this special attention, especially many first-time dog owners.

Videos put words into pictures; and for dog owners who are very visual, sometimes this can be a good source of additional information.

You need to find what is going to work for you. Maybe it will be a combination of things; a group class supplemented by a video or a book. Maybe a private lesson or two to get you over a rough spot. It's up to you!

Training should be fun for you and your dog.

Training Tools

Training tools are things you use to help you train your Yorkie. A leash is a training tool, as are collars. Your voice is a training tool. Anything you use during training can be considered a training tool.

Using Your Voice

I teach all of my training class students that they should consider their voice to be their ultimate and most important training tool. Their eventual goal—and yours with your Yorkie—should be to teach the dog to listen to you when you talk to him. That means he should come when you call him and stop sniffing the trash can when you catch him with his nose in it. You want your Yorkie to understand your words mean something and are not just noise.

To make it easier for your Yorkie to understand, you will be copying some of the mother dog's verbalizations—or at least her "tone of voice." When your Yorkie was still with his mom, he would interact with her and his littermates using verbal sounds as well as body language. If he wanted to play, his bark was higher in pitch. If a littermate or his mom responded to his play invitation, their barks were also higher in pitch.

We can make a safe assumption that play invitations are higher in pitch than the normal speaking voice, and we can use that to our advantage. When praising your Yorkie, say "Good boy!" in the tone of voice you used to say "Ice cream!" as a child. This should be higher in tone from your normal speaking voice but not as high pitched as a yelp that would mean hurt.

When your Yorkie was corrected by his mom, for example if he bit her with his needle sharp baby teeth, she would growl at him. That deep growl meant, "You made a mistake! Don't do it again." We can use this sound, too, to our advantage. When your Yorkie makes a mistake, you can use a deep voice to make a sound such as "Acckk!"

Bet You Didn't Know

Many women complain their dog listens to their spouse better than he does to them. Why? Men's voices are deeper and therefore carry more authority!

Now there is no way we can sound like a dog—even with lots of practice! Instead, what you are trying to do is use your voice in the same way that your Yorkie's mom used hers. Higher pitched for happy, very high pitched for hurt, and deeper sounding for correction. By using tones much like she used, you are hoping to minimize confusion during training.

Bet You Didn't Know

Around the house, I often whisper to my dogs. This teaches them to listen more closely to me.

If you are normally soft spoken and are concerned about using your voice to control your Yorkie, don't worry. Use your normal speaking volume (loudness) but vary the tones. You are teaching your Yorkie to listen to you, and if you are naturally soft spoken, that's fine. Your Yorkie can hear you very well.

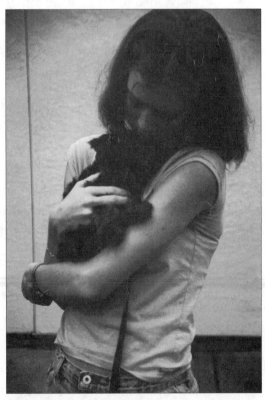

Use lots of praise and petting to reward your dog for good behavior.

Collars and Leashes

Collars and leashes are training tools, too, just as your voice is. Use collars and leashes a lot during the training process to teach your Yorkie to listen to your voice. Although we want him to understand that he should listen to you when you talk to him, he doesn't know that just yet, and the leash and collar can show him that he should listen to you.

Dog owners know they need a leash and collar when they take the dog out for a walk, but you should use them in other situations, too, such as when …

🏠 Your Yorkie acts up around the house, getting into the trash can or stealing the kids' toys, put the leash on his collar and keep him close to you.

🏠 The kids are playing and the Yorkie chases them, nipping at their legs, put the leash on him and prevent him from chasing.

🏠 The family is eating and the dog is trying to beg under the table, put his leash on him and make him lie down away from the table.

🏠 Guests come to the house, put your Yorkie on a leash so he isn't annoying your guests.

There are many ways to use the leash and collar; these are just a few examples. I will give you more ideas as we teach the basic obedience commands in the next chapter and as we discuss problem behaviors in the following chapter. Meanwhile, get used to using the leash and collar. Just remember to take it off your Yorkie when you can't supervise him; you don't want him to get it tangled up and choke himself.

Watch Out!

Always take the leash and training collars off your dog when you leave him alone. If left on him, they could become tangled and choke him.

Some of the training collars and leashes you might use can include the following:

- **Buckle collar.** A buckle collar is nylon or leather, fastens with a buckle of some kind, and holds your Yorkie's identification tags. This is the only collar many Yorkies will need. It is soft, gentle, and does not give much of a correction.

- **Training collar** (often referred to as a slip chain collar or choke chain). This collar works with a snap and release motion. Think of a bouncing tennis ball—snap (up) and release (down). *Never* jerk this collar hard and *never* hold it tight. Don't allow your dog to pull it tight, either, as it can choke your dog. When you use this collar to give a correction, always use your voice. "Acckk! No pull! (snap and release)." Otherwise your Yorkie may think the snap is simply a movement on your part without any meaning.

> **Watch Out!**
> Always—*always*—take the slip collar off of your dog when you cannot supervise him. This collar can choke your dog if he gets it tangled or caught on something.

- **Head halters.** These are much like a halter on a horse. They are very gentle and not used with any kind of snap or release; instead, use a gentle guiding motion. They can be found in sizes small enough for most Yorkies. Head halters are different from muzzles, although people unfamiliar with them may confuse the two.

- **Leash.** A leash, either one of regular length (4 to 6 feet) or a longer one, attaches to the collar or halter so that you have a means of using the collar or halter to teach your Yorkie. A collar alone won't do much; you must be able to use it, and that's where the leash comes in.

- **Rigid leash.** A rigid leash is an excellent tool for the owners of toy breed dogs. This is not a leash you will find at a pet supply store; you will have to make it yourself. At a pet supply store, buy an inexpensive lightweight cotton web or nylon leash. At a craft or hardware store, buy a 3-feet-long, $^3/_8$-inch in diameter, wooden dowel. Lay the leash up against the dowel, with about three inches of the leash, including the snap, hanging off the bottom. That will leave the loop for your hand hanging loose at the top. Using screws or wood staples, fasten the leash securely to the dowel along the entire length. If you want, you can wind duct tape along the length of the dowel for added security. This will give you a solid leash to help you teach your dog without having to bend to his height quite as often as you might otherwise need to do.

🏠 **Motivators and positive reinforcements.** These are things your Yorkie likes—they can be food treats, squeaky toys, furry toys, or even a tiny tennis ball. They can be used to help your Yorkie do what you want (as a lure, for example) or can be a reward for doing something right.

Use your training tools—no matter what they are—as much as possible. If you use the training tools only during training sessions, your Yorkie will think that they are for use only during training sessions and therefore the behavior he is learning during those sessions is also only for use at those times. Instead, use your training tools often during your daily routine.

Yorkie Smarts

To keep a motivator special, give it to your Yorkie only when you are working with him. Never give it to him "just because" or for no reason.

Teaching Your Yorkie

What do you do when your Yorkie does something wrong? Say, for example, you find toilet paper spread all over the bathroom and down the hall? This is a common Yorkie trick. If you are like many dog owners, the first thing you do is yell, "What did you do? Oh, bad dog! Shame, shame, shame!"

Now, did this teach your dog anything? Probably not. Oh, he may think you are unpredictable, or slightly unbalanced. He may think you dislike toilet paper. But I doubt very much he learned that he is not to unroll and shred toilet paper.

Why? Well, first of all, timing is critically important. If you caught him as he was pulling the toilet paper off the roll, you could then use your voice and scold him. But when you catch him halfway down the hall, with the roll already unrolled, it's too late. You have to catch him in the act.

In addition, you have to learn to prevent the problem from happening. Close the bathroom door or put up a baby gate so he can't get into the hall.

Keep in mind also that dogs do not learn what *to do* by being corrected. A correction can let the dog know when he made a mistake but it cannot tell the dog what to do instead. However, positive reinforcements do let the dog know when he did something right.

For example, let's look at the toilet paper problem again, applying what you've just learned:

- He's tearing up the toilet paper because it's fun.

- Prevent him from getting at the toilet paper as much as realistically possible.

- When you catch him in the act, correct him.

- When he comes into the bathroom with you and ignores the toilet paper, praise him and give him one of his own toys to play with.

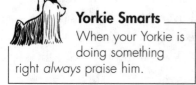

Yorkie Smarts

When your Yorkie is doing something right *always* praise him.

Much of your Yorkie's training can be approached in this manner. Let him know when's made a mistake but show him what he can do instead. Show him the right way and praise him enthusiastically for doing it.

The Agony of Negative Attention

Because so many dog owners respond to everything bad their dogs do by yelling, many dogs learn that doing things wrong is a sure way to get their owners' attention. These dogs will put up with any correction because it is still attention from their owner.

To change this scenario, the owner must focus on giving the dog attention for good behavior. This might be difficult in the beginning because the bad behavior cannot be corrected. (Remember, corrections are negative attention!) However, when the negative attention decreases and the good behavior is rewarded, the dog's focus will change.

Be Your Yorkie's Leader

I always stress leadership in my training classes. Puppies and young dogs naturally look to someone older for leadership just as young human children do. The parents and other adults are (or should be) natural leaders. Without leadership, the young would not grow up to know social rules and how to survive.

People who own larger breed dogs, especially those who can be quite powerful and dominant, seem to realize that they must assert themselves to be their dog's leader. Unfortunately, many small dog owners don't seem to understand that it's just as important for their dog.

Dogs are dogs are dogs—their size is immaterial. For good mental health, your Yorkie needs a leader and it must be you. If you don't assume the leadership position, your Yorkie will suffer for it. I have had (and will have more in the future) Yorkie owners call me with a whole list of their dogs' behavior problems. The dog urinates in the house, chews destructively, growls when the owner tries to do anything, sleeps at the head of the bed and growls when the owner moves, and a variety of other bad behaviors. The vast majority of these behaviors have developed because the dog is in charge; not the owner.

As the leader, you must make certain things happen:

- **Train your dog.** Be fair and as positive as he will let you be; but train him.

- **Be a confident leader.** If you are not yet confident about your role as leader, at least act like it!

- **Always eat first,** even if it's just a carrot. The leader of the pack always eats first and best.

- **Always go first.** Not only should you always go first because you are the leader, but Yorkies are tiny and easily stepped on. For his safety as well as your leadership position, make him wait for you to go through doorways first. Then give him permission to follow you.

- **Don't allow your dog to growl at you, ever!**

Most people add a dog to their family because they want a companion. Most people envision a dog like Lassie or Rin Tin Tin: a canine best friend. Your Yorkie can someday be your best friend, but first you must be his leader. Later, when your leadership is undisputed and when your Yorkie is well behaved and well trained, he can become your best friend.

Watch Out!

If your Yorkie growls at you, snaps, or tries to bite, call a professional trainer or behaviorist for help right away!

In the canine world, affection, leadership, and respect all go together. If you are not your dog's leader, you will not be respected and will be thought of as weak. Be a strong, confident leader.

Make Your Training Successful

You can make your training more successful by following a few guidelines. Remember, training shouldn't be something horrible that you dread doing. Instead, make it a part of your daily life and keep it upbeat and happy as you do the following:

- **Teach your Yorkie.** He wasn't born knowing what the word "Sit" means. So teach him. Show him what to do, help him do it, and praise and reward him when he cooperates.

- **Do not repeat commands over and over again.** That just teaches your Yorkie to ignore you. Plus, if you repeat it, which time counts? Which one should he respond to? Say a command once and then help him do it.

- **Be consistent.** Once you establish some rules—such as not dashing out open doors—you must consistently enforce them.

- **Praise your Yorkie** *as* **he is doing something right. Correct your Yorkie** *as* **he makes a mistake.** Praise and corrections that happen later are not effective.

- **Get everyone involved.** Everyone in the family should know how to train your Yorkie, and should consistently enforce the training rules.

Finish every training session with a success. Stop when your Yorkie has successfully learned something or when he does something very well. You and he will both finish the session feeling good. If your Yorkie is having a hard time with a particular lesson, ask him to do something you know he can do and can do well. After he does it, stop the training session there. You can then still stop on high note.

> **Watch Out!**
> Don't train your Yorkie when the pressures of the day will cause you to take out your frustrations on him.

No Excuses!

Don't make excuses for your Yorkie. Yorkies may be tiny, but they have fully developed brains and lots of terrier instincts. They are bright, alert, intelligent dogs who can and have thrived on training.

When teaching Yorkie owners, I often hear the following excuses:

- "He's so tiny, he can't do that." There is nothing in basic obedience that a Yorkie cannot do.

- "He can't go to a group training class; he's afraid of other dogs." Yorkies should not be afraid of other dogs. Sure, they can be cautious of strange big dogs; that's wise! However, Yorkies need socialization to other friendly dogs in a controlled situation.

- "I don't take him for walks because he's afraid." Again, Yorkies should not be fearful. The breed standard calls for an alert, self-confident dog. Your Yorkie needs to get to know the world so he can be confident. If he never leaves the house he will be afraid.

So no more excuses. Your Yorkie may be tiny, but he's still a dog! Treat him like one.

The Least You Need to Know

- Training has benefits for you, your family, and your Yorkie. It's something you all participate in.

- There are a variety of training techniques and tools.

- Teach your Yorkie by helping him do something right and praising him for it.

- You must be your Yorkie's leader before you can be his best friend.

15

The Eight Basic Obedience Commands

In This Chapter

- The importance of the basic commands
- Teaching those basic commands
- Using the commands at home and in public
- Tips for successful training

The eight basic obedience commands are: Come, Sit, Release, Lie Down, Stay, Watch Me, Let's Go, and Heel. These commands should be a part of every Yorkie's vocabulary. For pets and companions, these commands will help him be a nicer dog to have around the house, and will make life safer for him. For Yorkies who will participate in other dog sports and activities later, these commands are the foundation; advanced training will build upon them.

We will show you how these commands can be used around the house and out in public. For example, when your Yorkie will come when you call him and walk nicely on the leash, he's a joy to take out in public with you. When he knows how to sit and stay, you can also teach him not to dash out open doors. These eight basic commands are useful in many places in your life with your dog.

Let's Start with the Basics

Many Yorkies spend a great deal of time in their owner's arms or on their laps. These dogs don't learn the basic lessons that most puppies, especially larger breed puppies, must learn very early—the idea that their owner can control their actions. After all, when the Yorkie jumps up and down, the owner picks him up. When the Yorkie claws at a leg, the owner picks him up. It sounds like the Yorkie has control, doesn't it?

With the basic obedience commands, your Yorkie will need to learn that you can set some rules, ask him to do some things, and he should cooperate. Some dogs learn this very easily while others have a harder time with it. In any case, be patient. Remember, you are both learning at the same time.

Now, before we actually begin training, does your Yorkie know his name? When you say, "Pumpkin!" (for example) does he look at you? For a few days before you begin training, have some really good doggy treats and some special toys at hand and, every once in a while, simply say your dog's name in a very happy, upbeat tone of voice. After saying his name, toss him a treat or a toy and praise him!

Dog Talk

The eight basic commands are **Sit, Release, Lie Down, Stay, Come, Watch Me, Let's Go,** and **Heel.**

1. "Pumpkin!"

2. Toss the treat or toy!

3. Praise your dog in a happy tone of voice.

Pretty soon your dog will hear his name and turn toward you, waiting for something else to happen. And that is exactly what you want!

Teaching the Sit Command

Teaching your Yorkie to sit using the *Sit* command is relatively easy. Teaching him to sit still is a little harder, but we'll take this in small steps and set him up to succeed.

With the regular leash (not the rigid leash) on your Yorkie, lift him up on his grooming table or a chair. You want to be close to him at this point in training.

Hold his leash or collar in one hand so he doesn't jump off the table or chair, and have a treat in the other hand. Show him the treat. When he reaches up to sniff the treat, move it over his head toward his tail as you tell him, "Pumpkin, Sit." When his head comes up and back to follow the treat, his hips will go down. After he sits, praise him and give him the treat.

Dog Talk

Sit means lower your hips to the ground, keeping your front end up, and hold still.

If he spins around to try to get the treat rather than sitting, put the treat in your pocket. Put one hand on his chest where the chest and neck meet. Tell him "Pumpkin, Sit," and at the same time, push that hand slightly up and back (thereby pushing his chest up and back) as the other hand slides down his back toward the hips and tucks his hips down and under. Think of a teeter-totter; up and back at the chest and down and under at the hips. When he's sitting, praise him.

We want your Yorkie to understand that the word "Sit" means "put your hips on the ground, keeping your front end up, and be still." Now, obviously, you can't tell your Yorkie this and expect him to understand, so you must teach him that is what it means, and you can do this using your voice. When he does sit, praise him with a higher than normal tone of voice, "Good boy to Sit!" When he begins to move from position (not after he's gone) but as soon as he begins to move, use your growling tone of voice, "Acckk!" and put him back in the Sit position.

The Sit is a very useful command, not just as the foundation command for more advanced commands, but also for use around the house, as in the following situations:

- Have your Yorkie sit to greet people, especially if he likes to scratch their legs. He can't jump on people and sit at the same time.

- Have him sit when you hook up his leash to take him outside. If he's sitting, he can't be spinning around in circles out of excitement.

- When he wants you to play with him, have him sit first. Have him sit each time you go to throw his ball or toy.

After several days of practice, when your Yorkie is sitting each time you ask him to, you can move him to the floor. Hook up his rigid leash and place him on the floor in front of you. Stand up with a treat in hand, and ask him to sit. If he doesn't, tell him he made a mistake, "Acck!" and at the same time, move the end of the rigid leash (hooked to his collar) slightly up and back just as if your hands were on your Yorkie helping him. When he sits, praise him.

Bet You Didn't Know

Don't worry if you are a little clumsy with the rigid leash at first. It takes some practice getting used to it.

The Sit command is the foundation for all other commands.

Teaching the Release Command

Your Yorkie needs a beginning and an end to each command. The beginning is his name. When you say, "Pumpkin," he knows you're talking to him and he should listen. *Release* is a command that means, "Okay, you're done now, you can move." With this command, your Yorkie knows exactly when he's allowed to move from position.

With your Yorkie sitting either on the table or on the floor, tell him, "Release!" in a high-pitched tone of voice. Use the leash to gently move him from the sit.

Dog Talk

Release means "Okay, you can move now. You're done."

The primary purpose of the release command is to let your Yorkie know when he is free to move from a previous command. This alleviates confusion; he knows when he's done.

Teaching the Lie Down Command

Place your Yorkie on the table or chair, and hold the leash in one hand so he can't jump off. Have him sit. With a treat in one hand and another hand (the one holding the leash) on your Yorkie's shoulder, tell him "Pumpkin, *Lie Down*," as you let him sniff the treat. Take the treat directly to the ground in front of his front paws. (Lead his nose down with the treat.) As he starts to move down, the hand

Dog Talk

Lie Down means lie down on the floor or ground, and hold still.

on his shoulder can be assisting him in this downward movement. However, don't push! If you push, he may simply push back. When he's down, give him the treat and praise him.

When you're ready for him to move, give him the release command. With the leash, encourage him to move. The release from the Lie Down command should mean the same thing as the release from the Sit command, "You're done now. You can move."

The Lie Down command is very useful, both in the house and out in public. Use it in the following situations:

🏠 Have your Yorkie lie down during meals so that he isn't begging under the table. Place him where you can see him but away from the table.

🏠 Have him lie down at your feet or on the sofa next to you while you're talking to guests. He can't be jumping all over them or knocking their drinks over if he's being still.

🐾 Have him lie down and give him a toy to chew on when you would like to have some quiet time to read or watch television.

🐾 Have him lie down while you're talking to a neighbor.

🐾 Have him lie down while you get your mail out of the box and sort through it.

When your Yorkie will lie down well on command, with a minimum of help, begin practicing it with him on the floor. Hook up his rigid leash and place him on the floor in front of you. Give him the command to lie down and if he doesn't immediately begin to lie down, move the tip of the rigid leash down toward the floor, giving him a slight downward correction. When he lies down, praise him. When you're ready, release him and encourage him to move.

Teaching the Stay Command

The Stay command is used with the Sit and Lie Down commands. We want your Yorkie to understand that *Stay* means "remain in this particular position while I walk away, and remain here until I come back to you and release you." The Sit and Lie Down commands by themselves teach your Yorkie to hold that position until you release him; but only while you are with him. With Stay, you will be able to walk away from him.

Place your Yorkie on the table or chair, with the leash on him, and have him sit. Hold your hand in front of his face about two inches from his nose. Tell him "Pumpkin, Stay!" while you hold his leash in the other hand. If he moves, use your voice, "Acckk!" and put him back in position. Wait a few seconds (two or three seconds in the beginning) and then step back to him. Have him hold still while you praise and pet him, then let him know it's okay to move by using the release command.

Dog Talk

Stay means hold this position until I come back to you and release you.

After practicing the Stay command with the Sit command for a few days, try it with the Lie Down command. The training methods are the same except that you will be having your Yorkie lie down. However, you tell your Yorkie which action you want him to take. If you ask him to sit/stay and he decides to lie down, correct him and help him back up into a sit. He doesn't get to choose which command; you do.

Don't be in a hurry to move away from your Yorkie or to have him hold the stay for longer time periods. It is very difficult for puppies and young dogs to hold still, and right now it's more important that your Yorkie succeeds in his training.

Use the Stay around the house in conjunction with the Sit and Lie Down, as in the following situations:

- When guest come over, have your Yorkie lie down by your feet and tell him to stay. He cannot then be tormenting your guests!

- When you want him to stay away from the table while you're eating, have him lie down and tell him to stay.

- Tell him to sit and stay while you're fixing his dinner so he doesn't jump all over you and cause you to trip over him.

- Have him sit and stay at doorways, gates, and at the curb so you can teach him to wait for permission.

There are lots of uses for these commands. Just look at your house, your routine, and where you might be having some problems with your Yorkie's behavior. Where can the Stay command help you?

Teaching the Come Command

Come is a very important command—one that could potentially save your Yorkie's life some day. When I teach my dogs to come when called, I want them to understand that Come means "Stop what you're doing and come back to me right now, with no hesitation, as fast as you can run." This instant response might save your dog from a dangerous situation—perhaps an aggressive dog, an oncoming a car, or a snake in the grass. Situations come up every day that could cause your Yorkie harm; a good response to the Come command could save him.

With your Yorkie on the floor with his soft leash on, hold the leash in one hand and have some treats in the other. Back away from your Yorkie as you call him, "Pumpkin, Come!" Make sure you back up a few steps so he gets a chance to chase you. If he doesn't come to you right away, use the leash to make sure he does. Praise him when he does come to you, "Good boy to come!" and then give him the treat.

Dog Talk

Come means your Yorkie should go directly to you, without hesitation or detours, as fast as he can run!

Practice this also with a long leash. Regular long leashes can be too heavy for a Yorkie so try a lightweight rope. Just cut a 20-foot length of rope and fasten it to your Yorkie's collar. Practice the Come the same way you did on the regular leash. Keep the command, "Come," very positive as you call him.

Watch Out!

Never correct your Yorkie for anything after you have issued the Come command. Timing is vitally important, and if he misunderstands a correction, he could learn that coming to you is bad and results in a correction.

As your Yorkie learns the Come exercise and is responding to it well, add some games to the practice. Call him back and forth between two family members and offer him a treat each time he comes. Make sure you keep it fun and exciting.

If your Yorkie hesitates about coming to you—especially if something is distracting him—there are some tricks to make him come to you. First, don't chase him. That will only make him run farther and faster away from you. Instead, call his name in an exciting (not scolding) tone of voice and then run away from him. He will turn and chase after you!

Some other tricks will bring your Yorkie in closer to you. You can lie down on the ground, hide your face and call him. Or bend over and scratch at the ground as if you're looking at something very interesting. Ask your Yorkie, "What's that?" in an "Ice cream!" tone of voice. When he gets up to you, don't reach out and grab him saying "Ah ha!" You'll never fool him again. Instead, continue to talk to him in an excited tone of voice as you gently take hold of his collar and praise him for coming to you.

Watch Out!
Don't call your Yorkie to come and then scold him for something he did previously. Not only are late corrections ineffective, but you're teaching your Yorkie not to come to you. Make the Come positive and fun all the time!

The Come is a very important command.

Teaching the Watch Me Command

Training your Yorkie can be very difficult if you can't get him to pay attention to you. Most dogs will focus on their owner at home, but when out in public, they want to pay attention to everything but you! However, you can help your Yorkie succeed by teaching him how to pay attention.

When you tell your Yorkie the Watch Me command, you want him to look at you, your face, and preferably, at your eyes. Your Yorkie is to ignore the distractions and focus on you. Now, in the beginning, this focus may only last for a few seconds but later, as your Yorkie gets better at it and as his concentration gets better, he should be able to focus on you and ignore distractions for minutes at a time.

Dog Talk
Watch Me means pay attention to me and ignore distractions.

Place your Yorkie on the table or chair, with his leash in one hand to prevent him from jumping off. With your Yorkie sitting in front of you and with treats in one hand, tell him, "Pumpkin, Watch Me!" At the same time, let him sniff the treat, and then take it up to your chin. This movement and position is important. Let your Yorkie sniff the treat so he knows you have it. Take it up to your chin (slowly) so that as he watches the treat, his eyes follow your hand to your face. As he looks at the treat and then your face, praise him. After you praise him, "Good boy to Watch Me!" then pop the treat in his mouth. If he gets distracted and looks away, take the treat back to his nose and get his attention back to you.

Yorkie Smarts
Make sure you have a treat that your Yorkie really likes and then save that treat just for training sessions. Keep it special!

When your Yorkie will do this on the table or chair, place him on the ground. Hook up his rigid leash, and have him watch you.

If he doesn't, or if he does but then looks away, give a verbal correction, "Acck!" and a small snap and release of the leash. As soon as he looks back at you, praise him!

As your Yorkie learns the command, you can start making it more challenging. Tell your Yorkie, "Pumpkin, Watch Me!" and then back away from your Yorkie so that he has to watch you while you're both walking. When he can follow you for a few steps, back up in a zigzag pattern, making turns and corners. Back up quickly, then slowly. Add some challenges. Of course when your Yorkie can do this, and has fun following you, you should praise him enthusiastically!

Walking your dog is pleasurable when your Yorkie can walk nicely on the leash.

Teaching the Let's Go! Command

Good leash skills are necessary for all dogs. When on leash, the dog should respect the leash without fighting it, pulling on it, or choking himself on it. The *Let's Go* command will help teach those skills.

With your Yorkie on the soft (not rigid) leash, hold the end of the leash held in one hand, tell him "Pumpkin, Let's Go" and simply back away from him. If he watches you, praise him. If he follows you, praise him even more. However, if he sniffs the ground, looks away from you, or tries to pull in the other direction, use a snap and release of the leash and a verbal correction, "Acckk! No pull!" (Or say "no sniff!," if that's appropriate.) After the correction, if he looks back up to you, praise him.

Dog Talk

Let's Go means follow me on the leash, keeping it slack, with no pulling.

Back away from your Yorkie several times in several different directions. Each time he follows you and each time he looks up at you, praise him. Every time he pulls away, sniffs the ground, or ignores you, correct him.

Your goal is to have your Yorkie keep the leash slack as he follows you, paying attention to your every move. And when he does, you should praise him enthusiastically!

Teaching the Heel Command

We want the command "Heel" to mean "walk by my left side with your neck and shoulder area next to my left leg, maintaining that position no matter what I do." With that definition, if you walk fast, jog, walk slow, or simply amble, your Yorkie should maintain that position. If you go for a walk through crowd and have to zigzag through people, your dog should still maintain that position.

Teaching the Heel command requires a great deal of concentration on your Yorkie's part. Do *not* start teaching him to heel until he has been obeying the "watch me" command for several weeks (not days, weeks!) and has been doing the "Let's Go" command very well for at least two weeks with regular practice.

Place your Yorkie on the floor on the rigid leash. Hold the leash in your left hand and some treats in the right. Back away from your Yorkie as you tell him, "Pumpkin, Let's Go!" As he follows you, let him catch up with you as you back up slightly and turn so that you are facing the direction he is walking and he ends up on your left side. Walk forward together as you show him a treat and tell him, "Pumpkin, Heel!" Stop after a few steps, have him sit, and praise him as you give him the treat.

Repeat this several times, keeping each walking session short, enthusiastic, and fun. As he learns this command and is doing it consistently, begin making it more challenging by turning, walking quickly, walking slowly, and going different directions.

At this point in the training, with this method, always start with the "Let's Go" command and tell your Yorkie to heel as he arrives at your left side and you begin walking forward together.

After a week or two of this training, or when your Yorkie seems to understand what you want him to do, begin by having your Yorkie sit by your left side. Have some treats in your right hand, show him a treat and tell him, "Pumpkin, Watch Me!" When he's paying attention to you, tell him, "Pumpkin, Heel!" and walk forward. If he pulls ahead, use the leash to give him a snap and release correction as you tell him, "Acckkk! No pull!" When he slows down, backs off the pulling, and looks back to you, praise him and repeat the Watch Me command. When he watches you, praise him enthusiastically.

This requires a little more concentration on his part, so make sure you keep the sessions short, upbeat, and praise your Yorkie's successes.

When you take your Yorkie for a walk, don't ask him to heel the entire way. Instead, go back and forth between the let's go and the heel. Offer some variety and some challenge. However, once you start this training, do not let your Yorkie pull on the leash. Whenever he is on the leash, he is to respect it and never, ever be allowed to pull on it.

The Down Stay command is one you can use in many situations once your Yorkie knows it.

Tips for Successful Training

As I've already noted, your training will only be successful if you practice it regularly and use your training commands throughout your day. If the training is confined only to training sessions, your

Yorkie will think it applies only to those sessions. Instead, use these commands regularly, both in the ways I've already suggested and in other ways that are appropriate to your lifestyle. After all, my daily routine is not the same as yours, so we will use the commands differently.

Don't be embarrassed to practice your training out in public, too. If your Yorkie learns that you'll let him get away with bad behavior out in public, he'll take advantage, I guarantee it! Yorkies are smart enough to figure that out. So make him behave, even if once in a while you have to give him a firm, "Cut it out!" and a leash correction. Just make sure when he does behave himself he gets plenty of praise!

The Watch Me command teaches your Yorkie to pay attention to you.

Keep your training fun, too. If the training is serious and somber, neither one of you will enjoy it; and if you don't enjoy it, you aren't going to want to do it. Instead, have fun. Laugh with your dog, and in between exercises rub his tummy!

The Least You Need to Know

- The basic commands are the foundation for everything you will ever teach your Yorkie in the future.

- Teach your Yorkie the eight basic commands—Sit, Release, Lie Down, Stay, Come, Watch Me, Let's Go, and Heel.

- Keep your training session fun and upbeat but under control.

- Use these commands everywhere; not just in training.

Chapter 16

Yorkies Will Make Mistakes

In This Chapter

- 🏠 Why Yorkies get into trouble
- 🏠 How dog owners cause problems
- 🏠 Common behavior problems and solutions
- 🏠 How to handle additional canine problems

Being very small has its advantages. After all, if a Yorkie jumps up on someone, he may scratch their legs, but if a Golden Retriever jumps on someone, he could potentially knock them down.

However, even tiny dogs—even Yorkies—can develop some annoying behavior problems. Sometimes the problems are not the dog's fault; many times the owner is at least partially to blame. So let's take a look at why Yorkies do what they do, and what you can do about it.

Why Do Yorkies Get into Trouble?

Your Yorkie jumps up on you because he wants your attention or to be picked up. As far as he's concerned, that's not a problem. In fact, he's problem solving. He knows if he bounces up and down at your leg, you will reach down and pick him up. He has solved the problem of communication; he has taught you what he wants you to do. However, you may very well consider it a problem when he scratches your leg, or your grandmother's leg, or a child's face. You may also consider it a problem when he does it too often and becomes annoying.

We have to keep in mind when looking at problem behavior that these behaviors are not problems to the dog. Your Yorkie does things for a reason. We may not be aware of the reason, or we may not agree with what he's doing, but he knows exactly what he's doing!

Sometimes, though, other things can affect problem behavior—occasionally quite significantly.

Is Your Yorkie Healthy?

Poor health or changes in health can trigger changes in behavior. A urinary tract infection or incontinence can cause housetraining accidents. An infected tooth can cause a dog to chew on inappropriate things. If your Yorkie has a sudden abrupt change in behavior, schedule a visit to your veterinarian before attempting to correct the behavior. Tell your vet what has happened and that you want to make sure a health problem isn't behind it. If your dog gets a clean bill of health, then you can look at the problem from a behavioral viewpoint.

Many dog owners assume any behavior problem is rooted in bad behavior, but most experts feel that

Dog Talk

Behavior modification is the process of changing behavior. It combines training with an understanding of why dogs do things, and changing the dog, the owner, and the environment so the dog no longer behaves in a certain way.

at least 20 percent of all behavior problems—2 out of every 10 dogs—have a health-related issue behind them. That's why it's so important to see your vet first, before beginning any *behavior modification* training. It would be very unfair to punish your dog for behavior caused by a health problem—behavior he cannot control.

What Does Your Yorkie Eat?

Most Yorkies will thrive on just about any good quality food. After all, they don't eat very much! However, some dog foods that are more than 50 percent carbohydrates are known to cause a type of hyperactivity in some dogs—including Yorkies. Some good quality commercial foods are very high in cereal grains and, as we discussed in Chapter 11, this can cause some problems.

The most common symptom of food-related hyperactivity is exactly that, hyperactivity. The dogs affected by this can't hold still; they wiggle and bounce, jump and run, and are on the move until they're exhausted. They collapse, sleep, then wake up to do the same thing all over again.

If you suspect a food-related problem, read the label of the food you are giving your dog. Most Yorkshire Terriers do very well on a dry kibble food that is about 26 to 28 percent protein and 8 to 10 percent fat. Make sure most of the protein is from meat and not from grains and cereals. Feed your Yorkie a food that doesn't contain a lot of sugar and artificial preservatives, colorings, and additives.

Yorkie Smarts

If you switch foods, take your time. Add a little of the new food to the old and gradually—over two to three weeks—add more of the new food.

Is Your Yorkie a Lap Dog?

Of course your Yorkie is a lap dog; that's why you got a Yorkie! However, don't forget Yorkies are terriers! Terriers are active,

inquisitive, spunky dogs, and your Yorkie needs plenty of time to act naturally.

When your Yorkie doesn't get enough exercise, he may be restless, act like he can't hold still, or pace.

He may even act depressed. A dog who doesn't get enough exercise may also develop health problems, including obesity, diabetes, and heart disease. An overweight dog is not happy nor is he healthy. Regular aerobic exercise can help use up your dog's excess energy and keep his weight at a healthy level.

Bet You Didn't Know

The amount of exercise needed will vary from dog to dog. A nice four- to five-block walk around the neighborhood would be enough for a Yorkie puppy but a one-mile jog or a three-mile walk would be better for a full grown, healthy adult Yorkie.

Your Yorkie Needs Mental Stimulation

A bored Yorkie is going to find something to do to amuse himself, and you may not like what he chooses to do. You need to make sure you do something every day to keep his mind active and sharp; which in turn will help alleviate boredom. Try the following:

- Play games that make him use his mind. Hide and seek (having him find family members by name) or teach him the names of his toys.

- Practice his obedience training regularly.

- Get involved in a dog sport or activity so that he has something else to occupy his mind and body.

- Increase his exercise so that he's more likely to sleep when left alone.

- If he gets into trouble when left alone, give him a toy before you leave—a rawhide, a biscuit, or one of the new toys that dispenses treats as the dog plays with it.

🏠 Let him watch the birds at a bird feeder. You may be surprised at how much your Yorkie will enjoy watching the birds.

Are You the Leader?

Yorkies lacking leadership can develop a host of behavior problems. Leg lifting, marking, mounting, humping, and other unacceptable behaviors are frequently seen. Aggressive behavior toward family members is common, as is destructive behavior around the house. Food guarding, toy guarding, and similar behaviors are also common. A Yorkie who doesn't perceive his owner as his leader may try to assume the leadership position.

In your Yorkie's eyes, if you are not the leader, someone must assume the position! If you have not yet convinced your Yorkie you are the leader, you need to change how he regards his—and your—position in the family hierarchy. You can do this in a number of ways:

🏠 Play games that make him work for you; retrieving games and hide and seek games are good.

🏠 People should go through doorways and gates first. You go up and down stairs first. Make him wait for you.

🏠 Don't let him sleep in bed with you; he needs his own bed, although his bed should be in your bedroom.

🏠 Make him sit for everything he wants. Give him one command to sit and then help him do it.

Yorkie Smarts
Making your Yorkie wait for you in doorways and on stairways will help protect him so he doesn't get stepped on!

Watch Out!
If your Yorkie is an adult and thinks he's the leader and you are trying to change things, be careful. If you even think you could be bitten, hire a trainer or behaviorist to help you.

🏠 Feed him at set times, giving him his food and taking it away after 15 minutes. Do *not* free-feed, leaving food out all the time.

🏠 Think like a leader; be assertive and act confident.

How Do Dog Owners Cause the Problem?

As a dog obedience instructor, I watch dogs and their owners every day. I watch how dog owners interact with their dogs and I marvel at how well dogs get along in our world in spite of us! Unfortunately, we—the owners of dogs—are often the cause of behavior problems. And worse yet, the problems caused by the owners are the hardest to solve because it's harder to see problems within ourselves than it is to see the problems in our dogs.

The most common type of owner I see with Yorkies are the over-permissive owners. Overpermissive owners want to spoil their dogs and usually freely admit they spoil their dogs. Overpermissive owners don't set enough rules or, when they do set rules, they don't enforce them. These owners are not the dog's leader, and many problem behaviors can develop as a consequence.

Another type of owner that I often see with Yorkies is the over-protective owner. Overprotective owners are so concerned that something will harm their tiny dog that they don't allow the Yorkie to be a dog. By overprotecting their Yorkie, they take away his ability to cope with the world around him. By "protecting" him from every-thing, the dog often becomes fearful; sometimes aggressively fearful.

Bet You Didn't Know

Everything we do with our dogs causes them to react in some way. Watch your dog and see how he reacts to your emotions and moods.

I do occasionally see the owners who are overly demanding. De-manding owners would prefer the dog to be a furry robot that follows each and every order exactly as given. Dogs, of course, will make mistakes, and these owners will never tolerate mistakes. Yorkies belonging to these owners will never measure up no matter how hard they try.

Overly emotional owners are quick to get excited or quick to react and often end up with dogs just like them. Unfortunately, during episodes of excitement, these dogs—especially reactive Yorkies—can get out of hand.

Don't let your Yorkie learn bad manners or habits.

Making Changes

As we have seen, behavior problems occur for a variety of reasons. Food, exercise, boredom, your reactions to him, and your emotions can all play a part; as can his health. Your household routine and how dedicated you are to his training also play a part in his behavior.

There are so many different factors that lead to problem behaviors that trying to solve those problems can be challenging. However, it can be done.

So let's start at the beginning:

🏠 Make sure your Yorkie is healthy. Don't assume he is healthy; make an appointment with your veterinarian, and tell your vet why you are there.

🏠 Make and keep a regular daily schedule for training. Fifteen minutes of Sit, Lie Down, Stay, Heel, and Come—all on leash— will help keep his skills sharp and his mind attentive.

🏠 Continue your Yorkie's socialization. Make sure he meets different people, new dogs, and other animals. An isolated terrier is an unhappy terrier!

Yorkie Smarts ___
Preventing problems from occurring may mean limiting your Yorkie's freedom. Don't let him have free run of the house, and supervise him more closely.

Dog Talk ___
An **alternative behavior** is one that your Yorkie can do and be praised for that also prevents a problem behavior from happening.

🏠 Play with your dog every single day. Don't just toss the ball absentmindedly while reading the paper; instead, get down on the floor and play. The time spent with you is important, but so is the laughter!

🏠 Make sure your Yorkie gets enough vigorous exercise; every day, summer and winter. Participate in this exercise with your Yorkie.

🏠 Prevent the problems from occurring when you can. Put away the trash cans, pick up the children's toys, and put away the cushions for the lawn furniture.

🏠 Teach the dog an *alternative behavior.* He can't dash out the front door if he learns to sit at the door and wait for permission to go outside.

Common Behavior Problems and Solutions

Yorkies are, luckily, nice dogs and normally don't have a lot of behavior problems. Most jump up, and since they are so tiny, that's not usually a problem as far as many owners are concerned. Some Yorkies are barkers, and others like to dig. We'll discuss all of these problems and some others that are a little less common.

Mouthing and Biting

Yorkies are small, so many people don't seem to understand how important it is that they should never, *ever,* bite or even touch their teeth to skin or clothing. The Center for Disease Control in Atlanta, Georgia has declared a "dog bite epidemic" saying that more than 800,000 dog bite cases are reported yearly. When you consider that these are only the bites requiring medical attention, the numbers of actual bites are probably two to three times this number.

> **Watch Out!**
> If your dog bites someone, not only can your dog be killed, but depending on where you live, you can also face a lawsuit from the victim, medical costs, criminal charges, a fine, and possibly even jail time!

Every dog must learn that touching teeth to skin or clothing is absolutely forbidden. Ideally you should start teaching these lessons when your Yorkie is a puppy, but even older puppies and adult dogs can learn if you follow these simple rules:

🏠 Be consistent. Don't allow your Yorkie to bite you during play and then correct him for nipping in other situations.

- Don't allow your Yorkie to chase the children. There should be no nipping at their heels or clothing. Teach the children to play quietly with the dog; no running and screaming.

- Don't allow your Yorkie to grab at his leash, chew on it, mouth it, or pull against it with the leash in his mouth.

There are several ways to correct mouthing and biting. No one of these corrections is better or worse than the others; some are more useful in certain situations.

Use a squirt bottle with a solution of $\frac{1}{8}$ vinegar to $\frac{7}{8}$ water for those instances where the dog is nipping at your legs, heels, or clothes. Have the squirt bottle in hand in those situations (or times) when you know he is apt to do it. When he nips at your heels, squirt him as you tell him, "No bite!" When he backs off, praise him quietly, "Good boy."

If you have your hands on your dog, perhaps when hooking up his leash, playing with him, or petting him, and he tries to mouth or bite you, correct him right away without hesitation. With one hand, grab his buckle collar or the scruff of his neck (as a handle) and with the other hand simply close his mouth. Tell him firmly, "No bite!" Do not let go of his muzzle until he takes a deep sigh and relaxes. If you let go and he continues to try and mouth or bite you, close his mouth again, correct him again, and wait him out.

Watch Out!

It doesn't take much force to close a Yorkie's muzzle and keep it closed. One finger and the thumb can do it easily so be careful you don't hurt your dog while stopping the biting.

Yorkies Have Springs in Their Legs!

Yorkies jump up on people to be picked up. Your Yorkie knows that if he bounces up and down, looking really cute, and scratches at your leg, you will get the message and pick him up. You need to be aware that he is training you to do this, and you must stop the behavior.

First, don't pick him up when he's jumping and scratching. Then, teach your Yorkie to sit. This may seem very simple, but when the dog learns to sit before you pick him up, or sit for attention, including petting from you, he will sit in front of you, quivering in anticipation of petting, and will have no need to jump on you. If you consistently reward him for sitting, the jumping behavior will disappear.

You will also have to teach him to sit for other people. Use his leash and simply do not allow him to jump up. Have him sit first (before people greet him) and then, when he tries to jump, use a snap and release correction as you tell him, "No jump!" Make him sit, and don't allow other people to pet him until he's sitting. If you have a hard time making him hold the sit, use your rigid leash for this.

Bet You Didn't Know

Teaching your dog to sit instead of jumping up requires consistency in training. Everyone must make sure the dog sits; if someone is inconsistent, the dog will continue to jump up.

Prevent problems from happening as much as possible.

Barking

Yorkies are not normally problem barkers, but their high-pitched shrill bark can be annoying. A Yorkie who is allowed to continue barking can become a problem barker, and that can cause problems with neighbors.

Start correcting barking in the house when you are close. Make up a squirt bottle with about ⅛ white vinegar and the rest water. (You want just enough vinegar so you can smell it.) When someone comes to the door, for example, and your dog barks, walk quietly to the dog, tell him, "Quiet!" firmly but without yelling. Mist the vinegar water toward him. He will smell the vinegar, stop barking, back off and maybe even sneeze. When he stops barking, tell him, "Good boy to be quiet!"

Watch Out!

Use the squirt bottle on mist setting; not stream. A hard stream setting could hurt him if you hit him in the face or eyes.

If you yell at your dog to stop barking (most people's first reaction), you're doing the same thing he's doing—making lots of noise at the front door. To your dog, you're barking, too! So of course he isn't going to stop, he thinks you're the reinforcements!

However, when you quietly tell him to be quiet as you spray this nasty smelling vinegar water, he hears the command as you make it difficult for him to continue barking. Yorkies have a sensitive sense of smell and very few dogs enjoy the smell of vinegar. Make sure you praise him for being quiet when he does stop barking so that he knows when he's behaving properly.

Once your dog has learned what the word quiet means, start asking him to be quiet in other situations. Whenever he starts to bark inappropriately, tell him to be quiet, and make sure you back up your command. Again, always praise him for being quiet when he does.

If your dog barks when you're not home, you may have to set up a situation so you can catch him in the act. Go through all the motions of leaving: get dressed; pick up your purse, wallet, or briefcase; get in the car; and drive down the block. Park the car down the block and walk back with squirt bottle in hand. When your dog starts to bark, surprise him with a "Quiet!" and a squirt! If you set him up a few times, he will quickly learn that you have much more control than he thought!

Digging

Luckily, Yorkies are not normally problem diggers. Many will dig a small hole (usually in a corner or the garden) to bury a favorite toy or bone and some will dig a shallow hole to use as a nest. I usually recommend owners to allow these mild earth movements to happen; they are usually not very destructive and the dog usually keeps to the same place for a period of time.

If the digging has become annoying, however, you can control it by giving him his own spot to dig. A kid's sandbox full of dirt or potting soil works well. To show your Yorkie that the sandbox is his digging spot, take a half a dozen dog biscuits and stick them in the dirt so they are only partially covered. Invite your dog to find the biscuits and to dig here. As he finds the biscuits, completely bury a few so he has to dig for them and, in the beginning, help him do so. For the first few days, continue to bury something in this spot and invite him to find it. When he digs elsewhere, correct him and take him back to his spot; he'll learn.

Suggestions for Additional Canine Problems

Life is never boring when you live with a Yorkie, and that means Yorkie behavior can sometimes be unpredictable. You may let your Yorkie out in the backyard one day only to see him dig under the fence or try to climb over the fence. If (or I should say, when) your

Yorkie decides to try something new, don't panic. Stop, think about what he's doing, and then follow the steps we outlined above.

Here are a few suggestions for some specific behaviors:

- **Digging under the fence.** Bury some rocks in the holes he digs under the fence. Then try to figure out why he is digging under the fence. Make sure he's getting enough exercise, playtime, and attention from you.

- **Chasing cars or kids on roller blades, bikes, and skateboards.** Keep him on leash and when he tries to chase, correct him with the leash and have him sit. Enforce the Sit and Sit/stay command. If he can't sit still, turn around, walk the other direction and, if he doesn't walk with you, let the leash correct him. Praise him when he does walk with you.

- **Barking in the car.** Have him ride in the car in his crate. It's much safer for him that way anyway, especially when the crate is fastened in with a seat belt. If he still barks in the crate, use the squirt bottle. Squirt him as you tell him to be quiet. Praise him when he stops barking.

And never forget to praise your Yorkie when he behaves properly!

The Least You Need to Know

- Problem behaviors are not a problem to your Yorkie; they are very natural behaviors.

- Problem behaviors usually happen for a reason. Try to find out why your dog is doing what he's doing.

- Prevent problems from happening if you can; especially when you aren't there to teach him.

- When you are at home, teach him what is wrong and most important, teach him what is right!

Chapter 17

Understanding Yorkie Behavior

In This Chapter

- 🏠 Understanding the canine body
- 🏠 Understanding hunting dog behavior
- 🏠 Looking at the strange things dogs do
- 🏠 Common questions and answers about dog behavior

Have you ever wondered why your Yorkie does some of the things he does? Why does he sniff other dogs' feces? Why does your female dog mount a male dog? Why does he chase a shadow? Dogs can do some really strange things—at least strange to people—which can cause some misunderstandings. After all, most people get embarrassed when their dog tries to mount someone else's dog; it's not socially acceptable behavior! Yet, to your dog, it's very natural.

In this chapter, we'll take a look at some of the behaviors that confuse people. We'll also discuss some of those potentially disgusting behaviors dogs do—such as eating cat feces! Sometimes we don't know why dogs do what they do—after all, they can't tell us—but we can make some educated guesses.

How Dogs Make Sense of the World

The way dogs perceive the world and how they behave has a lot to do with how they are built. For example, we use our sense of sight for information about the world around us. Some dog breeds, including greyhounds and other sight hounds, use vision but many other breeds, including Yorkies, also depend upon their senses of hearing and smell for information about the world.

There are also physical characteristics that make dogs react in ways we don't understand. For example, their digestive systems often compel them to eat things that seem strange to us. In addition, their reproductive systems exert powerful forces on their behavior.

How Well Do Dogs Smell?

We can't even imagine how well dogs smell the world around them. Our noses are dull by comparison. Their highly developed sense of smell is why dogs are used so frequently by law enforcement agencies to detect drugs, illegal substances, bombs, and even poached animals and animal products. The ability to smell is also important to the Yorkie's original job as a rodent hunter.

If My Yorkie's Nose Is So Sensitive, Why Does He Roll in Stinky Stuff?

This is another habit that puzzles many dog owners. Why would an animal with such a sensitive nose roll in cow manure, rotting carcasses, or other stinky stuff? Although the dogs can't tell us why, some experts say that many predators, including dogs, roll in filth to help disguise their scent. Other experts say that the dog simply likes a particular scent—for whatever reason—because not every dog appears attracted to rotting carcasses. Some dogs will roll in cat urine, some will roll on tobacco products, and others appear attracted to petroleum products. Some dogs don't roll in anything! It seems to be a personal statement that some dogs make.

Why Do Dogs Pant Even When They Aren't Hot?

Dogs pant to lose heat. A dog can lose a lot of heat through the evaporation process on his wet tongue. Since dogs don't sweat anywhere except on the pads of their feet, this cooling process is very important.

However, panting is also a sign of stress. When in a situation that bothers him, for any reason, your dog may begin to pant. If he anticipates something happening at the veterinarian's office, your dog may begin to pant even though the air conditioning is on in the office.

Why Does He Yawn When He's Not Tired?

Yawning when not sleepy is what is called a calming signal. If during your training sessions, for example, your Yorkie looks away from you and yawns, he is trying to tell you to calm down. Apparently, he is feeling stress, either from himself or from you, and he's trying to relieve it. Other calming signals include eye blinking, sneezing, looking away, and scratching.

Why Does My Yorkie Eat Grass?

For many years, experts believed that dogs ate grass to cause themselves to vomit, since some dogs do vomit after eating grass. However, most dogs don't seem to have any trouble vomiting and will do so whenever something doesn't settle well in their stomach, so that explanation doesn't seem to make much sense. Instead, it seems that many dogs just like some plant material, and fresh, growing grass is attractive to them. When given a chance, many dogs (including mine) will eagerly consume tomatoes, strawberries, apples, carrots, and many other fruits and vegetables, especially sweet ones. Although dogs are scientifically classified as carnivores, behaviorally they appear to be omnivores—animals that consume both animal and plant matter.

Does One Year of a Dog's Life Really Equal Seven Human Years?

No, that's not really true. A one-year-old dog is roughly the equivalent (mentally, physically, and sexually) of a young teenage human. After that, each year of your dog's life roughly equals about five to seven years of human life. Yorkies will usually live 13 to 16 years; sometimes even longer.

Bet You Didn't Know

The individual personal scent secreted by the anal glands is also why dogs smell each other's feces. That personal scent tells them who this was.

Why Does He Lick His Genitals?

Although licking one's genitals doesn't seem to be an attractive behavior from a human perspective, it is a natural action for your Yorkie. Cleanliness is important to continued good health, and your Yorkie licks himself to keep himself clean.

Why Do Dogs Smell Each Others' Rear Ends?

This is another behavior that people don't appreciate but is very natural to dogs. Dogs have scent glands on either side of the anus. These glands, called anal glands, contain a scent that is unique to each dog. A small amount of scent is deposited each time the dog has a bowel movement. When greeting each other, dogs will take a sniff at these glands. Think of this as a personal perfume!

My Yorkie's Nose Is Not Cold and Wet—Is He Sick?

His nose should not be dry and chapped; if it is, call your veterinarian. However, a dog's nose feels cold because of the moisture that evaporates off the nose. His body temperature is actually higher than ours, so if there is no evaporation, his nose will feel warm to us.

Why Does My Yorkie Lower His Front End When He Wants Me to Play with Him?

When a Yorkie lowers the front end, including the head and shoulders, leaving the hips high, this is called a play bow. This body language is a natural expression of play and is used by dogs, wolves, coyotes, and many of the other canine species. Puppies will use this play invitation when they want their littermates to play with them, as well as with adult dogs and their human playmates, including you.

> **Bet You Didn't Know**
> If you wish to invite your Yorkie to play, you can use the same body language. Lift your hands high, then bring them down in front of you, making a bowing motion.

Understanding Hunting Dog Behavior

Yorkshire Terriers were bred to hunt vermin, specifically mice and rats. They had to have a good sense of smell and acute vision to find their prey, and then had to be quick and agile to catch it. Once the prey was caught, the dogs had to be tough enough to ignore any injuries the rats might cause them, and tenacious enough to kill the rats.

Today, Yorkies are still quick, agile, alert, tenacious little dogs. Movement of prey type animals will still attract their interest and, if a rat or mouse happens into your house, it had better look out! Take care with small pocket pets in your home such as hamsters or guinea pigs.

Hunting dogs have certain behaviors and characteristics that can be confusing to some dog owners. Let's take a look at some of them.

When I Walk My Yorkie Off Leash, He Sniffs Everything and Ignores Me. Why?

Your Yorkie is hunting. He shouldn't be off leash outside of a safely fenced-in yard until he's well trained enough to come when you call him even when he's hunting. Otherwise, leave him on a leash. If you want to give him more freedom, let him sniff and run on a long leash.

Why Does He Chase and Nip at the Kids?

He's reacting to their running and screaming. The kids' actions kick in what is known as the prey drive; the instinct to chase things that move and make noise. Since that is not how most children would like to play, and since nipping children is never acceptable behavior, you need to convince your dog that this behavior is not acceptable. Make sure the dog is supervised when the kids are playing and stop his chasing (and nipping) behavior *before* it starts. Use your leash to control him and use a verbal correction to let him know that he is not to chase the kids.

My Yorkie Keeps Trying to Get into the Hamster Cage. Does He Want to Play?

I doubt it! A hamster is an awful lot like a mouse or a rat and your Yorkie doesn't understand the concept of a pet rodent. Keep the hamster safe from your Yorkie and never leave the two alone together.

Why Does My Yorkie Lunge and Bark at Dogs We See on Our Walks?

There are many reasons for this. He may not have been socialized well enough to other dogs as a puppy, or perhaps he views other dogs as a danger. Yorkies can also be quite protective and may be trying to protect you. Last but certainly not least, as a hunting dog, he may feel he has to threaten the other dogs. Yorkies often have no idea how tiny they really are and how silly their threats are!

Looking at the Strange Things Dogs Do

Dogs do some weird things sometimes. We can guess at why they do some of these things while other times even the experts are puzzled. Let's take a look at some behaviors that mystify many dog owners.

Why Does My Female Yorkie Hump My Friend's Male Dog?

Your Yorkie is just expressing dominance over the male dog. There are many ways of showing dominance, and this is one way. Very dominant females will often continue this behavior into adulthood, mounting subordinate males during playtime. You can stop the behavior when it happens if it bothers you, but it is normal and is not related to a sexual act.

My Yorkie Likes My Cat!

Many dogs—even hunting dogs—and cats live happily together, especially when raised together. I have three cats and three dogs and have had dogs and cats together for many years. When the dog is taught as a puppy to respect cats and not to chase them, the two species can live together quite nicely.

My Yorkie Eats Cat Feces!

Ah, the cat litter candy problem! Cats evolved to eat prey, the whole prey, including skin, small bones, meat, and guts. Commercial cat food includes meat but also contains grains and grain products that cats often don't digest well. Therefore, they are often passing through only partially digested food and, your Yorkie, smelling this, thinks this is a wonderful treat!

When he helps himself, though, and you get all excited, it becomes a *really* exciting treat; because, after all, you are excited!

Put the cat litter box somewhere the cats can get into it but the Yorkie can't. Simple prevention is the cure here because you aren't going to change your cats' digestive system and the Yorkie is going to continue to search for kitty treats!

Common Questions and Answers About Dog Behavior

Yorkies are sensible animals and everything they do has a very good reason—to them! Let's look at some behaviors from your Yorkie's perspective.

Why Does My Yorkie Bury the Bone I Give Her?

Most dogs bury bones when they are through chewing them. Burying the bone hides it from other predators and protects it for future use. This behavior probably has its roots in hunting behavior; when survival depended upon what was caught during the hunt. Every scrap of meat or bone was important.

Why Does My Yorkie Still Pull on the Leash Even When He's Choking Himself?

Puppies aren't people, even though we've made them a part of our family, and they don't think like people. Your Yorkie is often so focused on going somewhere to see something, he isn't thinking about the discomfort on his neck. That's why we need to teach him to walk properly so he can go places without choking himself.

Why Is My Yorkie Constantly Jumping on My Legs?

What do you do when he jumps on you? Do you pick him up? He's training you quite nicely. He jumps on your legs, makes himself annoying, and you pick him up. That's exactly what he wanted. To stop him you need to stop picking him up when he's annoying, and then make him sit before you pick him up.

Your Yorkie jumps up because he is small and you are tall!

Why Does My Yorkie Want to Sleep with Me?

There is no reason why your Yorkie can't sleep in the room with you, but he needs his own bed. Not only is there a real danger of being squashed by you when he sleeps in your bed with you, but you each need your own bed. In bed with you, he will begin to think of himself as your equal, and he shouldn't. He needs to look at you as his leader.

Why Doesn't My Yorkie Pay Attention to Me When I Want Him To?

There are several things that could be happening. First of all, before you even start training, does your Yorkie get enough exercise? If not, paying attention to you could be hard. Does he get enough time with you when you aren't trying to train him? Playtime, time for grooming, and cuddling time are all important.

When you are training, use some really good food treats to teach the Yorkie to pay attention. Then keep the training sessions short and sweet so you aren't asking more than he can give you. Five minutes at a time is more than enough for most young Yorkies. With my dogs, I will train for a few minutes, then play with them. Then I will train again for a few minutes and finish up with another playtime. My dogs learn that their concentration and attention is rewarded by playtime.

The Least You Need to Know

- Dogs do things for a reason. We may not understand why, but they do.

- It's important we know as much about our dogs as we can so that we can make both our lives more enjoyable and safer.

- Yorkies were originally hunting dogs and retain many of those instincts. This does affect their behavior.

- If any behaviors escalate into aggression (toward people or other animals) it's time to call in a professional trainer or behaviorist for help.

A Doggy Dictionary

aggression   A hostile reaction to stimuli. It can be directed toward people, dogs, or other things. Aggression is the fight part of the fight or flight instinct.

agility   An obstacle course for dogs that can be used for fun training and confidence, or as a competitive sport.

allergies   An allergy is when the body reacts to a substance that is touched, inhaled, or eaten. The body then releases histamines (hence an antihistamine to treat it).

alternative behavior   Any action (or inaction) you train your dog to perform in order to prevent an unwanted behavior.

American Kennel Club (AKC)   The AKC registers litters of puppies and individual dogs, and sanctions dog shows and other dog events.

body language   Your dog's use of body position; ears, tails, and legs; and facial expressions to communicate.

bonding   A feeling of deep commitment or attraction between dog and owner; a responsibility toward each other.

boundary training   Teaching the dog to remain within and to respect boundaries.

buckle collar A nylon, cotton, or leather collar that fastens with a buckle; not a slip type collar.

Canine Good Citizen A program administered by the AKC to promote good canine citizens and responsible owners.

cardiac pulmonary resuscitation (CPR) An emergency first-aid procedure to keep the dog's heart beating and to keep breath in him.

choke collar A training collar, works with a snap and release motion.

Come An obedience command for the dog to stop everything and go directly to you.

conformation competition Dog shows for evaluating a dog as compared to others of his breed and in accordance with the breed standard. Also called conformation championship.

correction Verbal or physical acknowledgement of a mistake.

cue A command or signal.

distractions Things that can break the dog's concentration.

dominance Levels of comfort within the pack or family.

earth dog Same as go to ground; field trials for terriers in which the dog goes into a tunnel after prey.

emergency A medical or veterinary term that means something is potentially life threatening and can't wait until the next business day.

exercise Physical activity or movement.

fearful aggression An aggressive reaction, by a shy or timid dog, that is caused by fear.

field trial A trial or evaluation for dogs used for hunting.

force Making the dog do something by using physical strength; or by using mental or leadership strength to cause the dog to cooperate.

go to ground Field trials for terriers in which the dog goes into a tunnel after prey.

group classes   Small group situations where dogs and their owners are taught by an obedience instructor.

halter   A training tool that fits over the dog's head much like a horse's halter. It can be used in place of a training collar.

heartworm   A parasitic worm that lives in the heart; left untreated it causes death.

Heel   An obedience command for having the dog walk by your left leg.

hookworm   An intestinal parasite.

housetraining   Teaching the puppy or dog to relieve itself outside or in a specific place; not indiscriminately in the house.

instinct   Inborn urges to respond to things in a specific manner.

leash awareness   Teaching the dog to be aware of the leash and to respect the leash.

Let's Go   An obedience command for walking nicely on the leash without pulling; but not in the Heel position.

long line   A longer length of leash or clothesline rope used to teach the come command and for boundary training.

lure   Something to encourage the dog to follow, to be shaped into position, or to do something.

Lyme disease   A tick-transmitted disease.

mimic   To learn by watching and then copying another's actions.

motivation   A dog's desire to do something or obey a command; can be influenced by providing a lure and a reward.

motivator   A reward or lure for doing something right.

negative attention   Corrections that are purposely sought by the dog (by misbehaving) as a means of getting attention from the owner.

parasite   An organism that lives off another.

positive reinforcement   Anything used to encourage a dog to continue behaving or obeying commands; can include verbal praise, petting, food treats, and toys.

praise   Verbal affirmation, approval.

shaping   Using a training tool to help the dog do what is wanted; shaping into position.

Sit   An obedience command; having a dog assume the sitting position.

socialization   The process of introducing puppies to different people, dogs, animals, sights, sounds, and smells.

Stay   An obedience command for having a dog hold his position without moving.

submissive   Showing respect for dominance.

temperament   Personality and character.

therapy dogs   Trained and certified dogs who visit people in nursing homes and hospitals.

time out   Time away in a quiet spot; breaks the thought processes. Good for dogs who are misbehaving.

toy breed dogs   The AKC recognizes several breeds of dogs that compete in dog shows in the toy group. These are all tiny breeds and include the Yorkshire Terrier as well as Chihuahuas, Papillons, and other well-known tiny breeds.

toys   Dog toys are items—either commercial or home made—that the dog can play with and chew on.

training tools   Anything that is used to train the dog; including leash, collar, voice, and food treats.

vaccination   Injections that encourage the body to develop antibodies to protect from a particular disease.

Wait   An obedience command for holding still and waiting for another command.

Yorkies (and Other Dogs) on the Internet

The Internet is a wonderful research tool for all dog owners. Yorkie owners can find some enriching sites on the Internet. If you're looking for Yorkie breeders, Yorkie jewelry, books on Yorkies, or Yorkie clubs, you can find them all on the Internet.

Be cautious, however. Never assume that everything you read on the Internet is correct. Anyone can post a web page, and while there is good information out there, there's also a lot of garbage! Don't hesitate to ask questions, and always look into who is doing the writing.

Yorkie-Specific Sites

www.hoflin.com/BR/Yorkshire%20Terriers
Yorkie breed description and ratings by owners

www.petcrest.com/yorkiehi
Pet crest (shield design) for the Yorkie

www.barkbytes.com/history/yorkie
Yorkie history

www.akc.org/breeds/recbreeds/york.cfm
AKC Yorkshire Terrier breed standard

www.k9web.com/dog-faqs/breeds/yorkies
Frequently asked questions

www.yorkierescue.com
Yorkshire Terrier National Rescue, Inc.

Nutrition, Health

www.petinsurance.com
Veterinary Pet Insurance

www.navigator.tufts.edu
Nutritional Navigator; more information about nutrition

www.quackwatch.com
A site about human medicine designed to help people avoid false information. It's very informative for dog owners, too.

www.petnet.com
The Pfizer Animal Health website; information about pet health care

www.goodpet.com
Dr. Goodpet Laboratories; natural pet products

www.canidae.com
Canidae Pet Foods

www.hillspet.com
Hill's Pet Nutrition, Inc.

www.iamsco.com
Iams Co. dog and cat foods

www.naturzchoice.com
Nature's Choice dog foods

www.petconnect.com/nutro
Nutro products

www.purina.com
Purina animal foods

www.waltham.com
Waltham pet foods

General and Miscellaneous Information

www.kitten.com/dogs
The Purina dog and cat pages have a lot of different information of interest to dog owners, including grooming information.

www.cbs.com/lateshow/ttlist
Search for dogs and you'll get David Letterman's top 10 lists concerning dogs.

www.canismajor.com/dog/guide
Dog Owner's Guide

www.dualcom.com/books/dogs
Books about dogs

www.amazon.com
A big bookstore with lots of books about dogs

Dog Supplies

www.canineequip.com
Canine equipment

www.foxandhounds.com
Dog collars

www.blueribbonpet.com
Blue Ribbon Pet Supplies

www.cardinalpet.com
Cardinal Laboratories; pet supplies, including shampoos

www.coastalpet.com
Coastal Pet Products; supplies

www.dogwise.com
One of the best sources for dog books

www.happydogtoys.com
Happy Dog Toys

www.kongcompany.com
Kong Co. toys

www.4dogs.com
Supplies and treats

www.jbpet.com
J-B Pet Supplies

www.jandjdog.com
J & J Supplies; competitive obedience and agility supplies

Index